HERESIES

John Gray

Granta Books

London

Granta Publications, 2/3 Hanover Yard, London N1 8BE

First published in Great Britain by Granta Books 2004

A CIP catalogue record for this book
is available from the British Library.

1 3 5 7 9 10 8 6 4 2

Typeset by M Rules

Printed and bound in Great Britain
by Bookmarque Limited, Croydon, Surrey

CONTENTS

CONTENTS

ACKNOWLEDGEMENTS

The essays collected in this book were published over a period of years in the *New Statesman*. I am grateful to Peter Wilby for commissioning the series. I could not have had a better Editor, or one more tolerant of heresy.

INTRODUCTION

The twentieth century was an age of faith, and it looks as if the twenty-first will be as well. For much of the century that has just ended, the world was governed by militant political religions, each promising paradise on earth. Communism promised universal freedom and prosperity; it succeeded only in adding another chapter to the history of human misery. After the fall of the Berlin Wall, the cult of the free market promised all that communism had failed to deliver. The neo-liberal era lasted little more than a decade. The post-Cold War interregnum was shattered by the attacks on Washington and New York, and the American attempt to export democratic capitalism worldwide is meeting a brutal end in the killing fields of Iraq.

Both communism and neo-liberalism were messianic movements, using the language of reason and science, but actually driven by faith. Seemingly deadly rivals, the two faiths differed chiefly on a point of doctrinal detail – whether the final perfection of mankind was to be achieved in universal socialism, or global democratic capitalism. Just as Marx's revolutionary socialism had done, the global free market promised an end to history. As could have been foreseen, history continued – with an added dash of blood.

Like most Enlightenment ideologies, communism and

neo-liberalism were obsessively secular. At the same time they were deeply shaped by religion. Looking to a future in which all of mankind would be united in a single way of life, each was rooted in a view of human history that is found only in western monotheism. Marxism and the cult of the free market are only the latest in a succession of Enlightenment faiths, in which the Christian promise of universal salvation reappears as a political project of universal emancipation.

For the pagans of pre-Christian Europe, history was an unending succession of cycles, no different from those in the natural world. In contrast, in western monotheism – in Judaism, Christianity and Islam (which in this respect belongs in the West) – salvation is the culmination of history. Judaism was concerned with the destiny of a particular people, not the species as a whole; the missionary impulse was absent. With the coming of Christianity, monotheism became universal in its claims. It is a development that is commonly seen as an advance. Yet it was this transformation that sowed the seeds of the militant political religions of modern times

The thinkers of the Enlightenment saw themselves as reviving paganism, but they lacked the pagan sense of the dangers of hubris. With few exceptions, these savants were actually neo-Christians, missionaries of a new gospel more fantastical than anything in the creed they imagined they had abandoned. Their belief in progress was only the Christian doctrine of providence emptied of transcendence and mystery.

Secular societies are ruled by repressed religion. Screened off from conscious awareness, the religious impulse has mutated, returning as the fantasy of salvation through politics, or – now that faith in politics is decidedly shaky – through a cult of science and technology. The grandiose political projects of the twentieth century may have ended in tragedy or farce, but most cling to the hope that science can succeed where politics has failed: humanity can build a world better than any that has existed in the past. They believe this not from real conviction but from fear of the void that looms if the hope of a better future is given up. Belief in progress is the Prozac of the thinking classes.

In science progress is a fact, in ethics and politics it is a superstition. The accelerating advance of scientific knowledge fuels technical innovation, producing an incessant stream of new inventions; it lies behind the enormous increase in human numbers over the past few hundred years. Post-modern thinkers may question scientific progress, but it is undoubtedly real. The illusion is in the belief that it can effect any fundamental alteration in the human condition. The gains that have been achieved in ethics and politics are not cumulative. What has been gained can also be lost, and over time surely will be.

History is not an ascending spiral of human advance, or even an inch-by-inch crawl to a better world. It is an unending cycle in which changing knowledge interacts with unchanging human needs. Freedom is recurrently won and lost in an alternation that includes long periods of anarchy and tyranny, and there is no reason to suppose that this cycle will ever end. In fact, with human power increasing as a result of growing scientific knowledge, it can only become more violent.

The core of the idea of progress is the belief that human life becomes better with the growth of knowledge. The error is not in thinking that human life can improve. Rather, it is imagining that improvement can ever be cumulative. Unlike science, ethics and politics are not activities in which what is learnt in one generation can be passed on to an indefinite number of future generations. Like the arts, they are practical skills and they are easily lost.

Many Enlightenment thinkers accepted that scientific advance might slow down or stop, as in previous periods of history, and in that case social progress would stall as well. Yet so long as the advance of science continued, they believed human life would improve. The improvement might not be quick or steady, but it would be incremental, with each new advance building on the last, like the growth of knowledge in science. What none of the thinkers of the Enlightenment envisaged, and their followers today have failed to perceive, is that human life can become more savage and irrational even as scientific advance accelerates.

Now that science is worldwide the advance of knowledge is unstoppable. Short of an almost unimaginable global crisis there is no prospect of the advance of science slowing or going into reverse. In ethics and politics, however, no gain is irreversible. Human knowledge grows, but the human animal stays much the same. Humans use their growing knowledge to promote their conflicting goals – whatever they may be. Genocide and the destruction of nature are as much products of scientific knowledge as antibiotics and increasing longevity. Science enlarges human power. It cannot make human life more reasonable, peaceful or civilized, still less enable humanity to remake the world.

In calling belief in progress an illusion, I do not mean that we should – or could – simply reject it. When Freud described religion as an illusion, he did not imply that it was wholly false, nor was he suggesting that humanity could do without it. Illusions are not mere errors. They are beliefs to which we

4

cling for reasons that have nothing to do with truth. We turn to religion not for an explanation of the universe, but in order to find meaning in life.

The illusion of progress has sometimes been benign. It inspired some genuine social advances, such as the abolition of judicial torture. (Ironically, as I note in Chapter 15, some American liberals are now arguing for its reintroduction.) Even so, I believe it has now become harmful. Whatever role it may have had in the past, belief in progress has become a mechanism of self-deception that serves only to block perception of the evils that come with the growth of knowledge. In contrast, the myths of religion are ciphers containing the truth of the human condition.

In order to be effective, illusions must be genuinely believed; but it seems that even its most militant evangelists today secretly suspect progress to be an illusion. How else can we explain their anxious certainty? At least since Pascal, religious faith has thrived on doubt. No trace of doubt leavens the dogmas of secular humanism. They are too brittle to withstand serious questioning.

Anyone who dares question the idea of progress is at once accused of wishing to return to the Dark Ages. Yet it is a fact that the largest mass murders in history were perpetrated by progressive regimes. Old-fashioned tyrants may have murdered on a large scale – though nowhere near that of recent times; but it is not the scale of modern mass murder that is its most distinctive feature. It is the fact that it was done to elevate the human condition. The millenarian movements of the late Middle Ages were sometimes violent, but they did not see violence as the instrument whereby a new world would be forged – that task was left to God. Even the Inquisition, which killed and tortured in the belief that it was saving souls, did not claim that it was building an earthly paradise. It is only in modern times that mass murder has been seen as a means of perfecting humanity.

Lenin boasted of being an 'engineer of souls', who was able to construct a new 'socialist humanity'. The end-result of the Bolshevik experiment was mass murder and broken lives on an unprecedented scale. The scale of death in Soviet Russia was rivalled only in Maoist China, another progressive regime. The Nazis despised Enlightenment values of freedom and toleration; but they shared the Enlightenment goal of using science to alter the human condition. Like Lenin, Hitler dreamt of creating a new type of human being. Mixing Nietzsche's childish brew with the deadly poison of 'scientific racism', he perpetrated a uniquely atrocious genocide.

The lesson of the century that has just ended is that humans use the power of science not to make a new world but to reproduce the old one – sometimes in newly hideous ways. This is only to confirm a truth known in the past, but forbidden today: knowledge does not make us free.

We inherit from Greek philosophy the belief that knowledge is liberating, but the biblical myth of the Fall is closer to the truth. The increase of knowledge brings many benefits; but it is not an unmixed good. Tempting humanity with the promise of magnifying its power, it ends by enslaving us.

In modern times, nothing is more heretical than the idea that knowledge can be a sin, and it is this thought that inspires the essays that are collected here. The belief that humanity advances with the growth of knowledge is at the heart of liberal humanism. In many ways humanism is not much more than secular Christianity; but it has suppressed the profound insights into the contradictions of human nature and the ambivalence of knowledge that were preserved in the Christian tradition. At the same time it has perpetuated Christianity's worst errors.

Among the world's religions Christianity has always been one of the most radically anthropocentric. Christians believe humanity is separated from the natural world by an impassable gulf; other animals exist to serve us. It could be argued that the biblical account in which God grants man dominion over other species implies a duty of care to them – a view held by the Franciscans, who believed that other animals have souls just as humans do.

Nevertheless, the idea that humans are supremely valuable in the scheme of things has always been at the core of Christianity, and it is no less central in secular thought. The peculiar notion that human personality is the source of all that is valuable in the world makes little sense once it is wrenched from a theology in which humans are made in the image of a divine person. Despite that, it has become the basis of humanism.

In several of the essays in Part 1 of this book, I explore the ironies of secular thought. Humanists like to represent themselves as ardent admirers of the human animal. Yet – as I show in Chapter 4 – religion is a human impulse as natural and universal as sex. In intellectual terms atheism is a Victorian fossil. In Freudian terms it is a form of repression. In seeking to eradicate religion from human life, humanists are trying to suppress a basic human need. As with sex, repression does not work. The religious impulse returns, often in perverse and grotesque forms, such as humanism itself.

The theistic belief that humanity has been given dominion

over the world has not been relinquished. It has been recycled as the humanist belief that, by using the power of science, humanity can escape the natural laws that govern all other animals. In Chapters 6 and 7, I show how the belief in human supremacy is running up against the finitude of the Earth's resources. Science teaches humility. Humans cannot evade the laws of thermodynamics, and there is nothing about progress in Darwin's theory of natural selection. It is industrialization that has enabled humans to attain their present numbers; but worldwide industrialisation is the basic human cause of climate change, and the effect of global warming is to make the planet less hospitable to humans. Nothing that humans can do can prevent the Earth returning to equilibrium.

In the minds of secular believers, however, we can overcome the laws of nature: science can make us as gods. One expression of this attitude is the practice of vivisection. In Chapter 8 I examine the way in which animals have become sacrificial victims of the cult of science.

Liberal humanism is a secular rendition of a Christian myth, but the truth in the myth has been lost on the way. The biblical story of the Fall teaches that evil cannot be rooted out from human life. Humans are radically flawed – a perception expressed in the doctrine of Original Sin. It is not error or ignorance that stands in the way of a better world. The human animal may yearn for peace and freedom, but it is no less fond of war and tyranny. No scientific advance can alter the contradictions of human needs. On the contrary, they can only be intensified as science increases human power.

In Part Two, I consider the type of thinking that led to the catastrophe that is unfolding in Iraq. Like the other essays in this volume, they have been only lightly edited. Nothing of substance has been altered; the analysis and forecasts remain just as they were on first publication (whose date is given at the end of each essay). They show that the disasters flowing from the war were not – as its defenders now claim – beyond the power of reasonable foresight. In Chapter 10 (March 2002), I note that 'toppling Saddam might lead to the fragmentation of the Iraqi state' – a warning repeated in Chapter 12 (August 2002). In Chapter 14, published in January 2003, I observed: 'With overwhelming force at their disposal, the confidence of American military planners that the present Iraqi regime can be destroyed without much difficulty may prove to be justified; but the bland optimism of America's civilian leadership regarding the costs and risks of reconstructing Iraq in the aftermath of war is desperately deluded.' Published on the eve of war in March 2003, Chapter 16 points to the risk that 'the Iraqi state, a rickety structure cobbled together by departing British civil servants, will fracture and fragment in Yugoslav or even Chechen fashion.' In Chapter 18, written in April 2003, just after the fall of Baghdad, I write: 'The reality is that the war has not ended but instead entered a new phase. Iraq's would-be liberators are now the targets of Chechen-style guerrilla resistance from sections of Iraq's diverse and fractious populations'. My reason for rehearsing these fore-casts is not to claim any special prescience, but to show that the course of events was predictable. There were many similar predictions by opponents of the war – a group that included nearly all experts on arms control. All were ignored. As I note in Chapter 19 (August 2003), the Iraq war 'was fought for reasons that were never stated. As a result, it has never had democratic legitimacy.' The precise course of events that produced the war may not be known for some time, but it is clear that WMD were a pretext for a decision to go to war that was made on other grounds.

For some of those who planned the war, it was an exercise in *realpolitik*, with Iraqi oil the prize. For others it was a form of apocalyptic politics pursued by military means. In the aftermath of 9/11, neo-conservative intellectuals gained an influence in American government they had never had before (much of which they have since lost). For these radical ideologues, invading Iraq was a means of reshaping the Middle East – and eventually the world – in an American image.

Not the least of the ironies of the present time is the fact that the neo-conservatives – consumed with hatred for all things European – are evangelists for European radical ideas. Like the French Jacobins, they aim to remake the world – and are ready to spill large amounts of blood in the attempt. Like Lenin, they see the world in apocalyptic terms. In their view, history is a record of bitter struggles, but these conflicts are only a prelude to a new world in which a single form of government is destined to prevail universally.

The most striking development in politics in the past two decades is that this apocalyptic mentality has gone mainstream. In the past it was confined to revolutionary movements and totalitarian regimes. With the collapse of communism, naïve thinkers expected a revival of a more sceptical, pragmatic style of politics. In fact the apocalyptic turn of mind – once the prerogative of the Left – found a new home on the Right.

It was a mix of millenarian fantasy with inept *realpolitik* that produced the war in Iraq. In the policies of Bush and Blair, apocalyptic hopes jostle with cold-blooded – if often mistaken – geo-political calculation. Dr Strangelove has joined forces with Dr Billie Graham. The result has been black farce on a grand scale.

The regime of Saddam Hussein was extremely repressive, but it was certainly not fundamentalist. It was a tyranny on a western secular model – that of the Stalinist Soviet Union. In the Islamic countries of the Middle East, secular regimes survive only if they are highly authoritarian; democracy means a sort of popular theocracy, as in Iran. When they demolished the regime of Saddam Hussein, Bush and Blair consigned Iraq – or rather the Shia-dominated state that will emerge from civil war and the break-up of Iraq – to religious rule. At the same time, they empowered the forces of Al Qaeda throughout the world.

Al Qaeda has more in common with the Baader-Meinhof Gang than with the mediaeval Assassins. Like the Jacobins and Bolsheviks, it acts on the apocalyptic belief that the human condition can be transformed by terror. For that reason alone, it belongs in *our* world, not the mediaeval past.

If the twentieth century was a time of political faith and state terrorism, the twenty-first looks like being one shaped by religious fundamentalism and privatized terror. At present, the most dangerous forms of terrorism are the work of radical Islam. That will not always be so. A generation or so from now, Al Qaeda may have been replaced by cults like the Aum movement, which planted poison gas on the Tokyo underground. Both are animated by the peculiarly modern belief in the regenerative power of spectacular violence.

Al Qaeda's threat is real. However much it has been strengthened by mistaken policies, terrorist violence cannot be tolerated. Even so, it cannot be eliminated.

The 'war on terror' is another version of the secular faith in the evanescence of evil. Not so long ago, much of what is now routinely described as terrorism was seen as insurrection or civil war, and accepted as part of the normal instability of politics. An intelligent policy would aim to separate these regional and local conflicts from the activities of Al Qaeda, which is unique in being a global network. The aim would be to return terrorism to more historically normal levels.

Given patience, such an approach could be significantly more productive than current policies, but it would require a massive scaling-down of expectations. Political life would have to undergo a mutation in which it was emptied of apocalyptic hopes. From being a grand project driven by millenarian fantasy, politics would become a succession of modest expedients. Instead of being a vehicle for a vision of a new world, it would be a way of coping with the recurring evils of the human condition.

Such a transformation would be highly beneficial. It is also extremely unlikely. The hope of a better future may be shaky, but it is the only faith many people have left. Lacking any genuine religion, they cannot accept the truth that the future will be little different from the past. As a result, we can be certain that it will be the same. Over the next few decades, the anxious secular faith in progress looks set to meet the apocalyptic violence of radical Islam in an opaque and savage conflict.

Part Three looks directly at politics today. Received wisdom tells us that the far right is an atavistic movement, which only advances in response to economic crisis; but in continental Europe, it has come to prominence in conditions of prosperity and – in Austria – of full employment. In Chapter 20, I argue that Europe's new far right is – like its predecessors between the wars and radical Islam today – thoroughly modern. To believe that its advance will be curbed by further 'modernization' is to delude oneself.

Of all contemporary politicians, Mr Blair has identified himself most closely with the illusions of modernization; but reality tends to break in despite the most careful management of the media. Iraq has destroyed the neo-conservative fantasy of modernizing the Middle East on an American model – and with it Mr Blair. Whether or not he continues in office up to the next general election, he has no future in politics. Perhaps he will follow Michael Portillo – also a pious modernizer – into the media, showing that politics really is now not much more than a branch of the entertainment economy, as suggested in Chapter 24.

Our political ideas mirror our conceptions of time and knowledge. The idea of progress, which animates all parties today, is a hollow replica of a Christian conception of history. In a Christian view, history cannot be without meaning. It is a tale of sin and redemption written by God – even if much in it is bound to remain mysterious. The risk of any historical religion is that it ends by giving too much importance to time and too little to that which is eternal. Traditional Christianity – the faith of Augustine, for example – sought to avoid this danger by denying that the workings of providence can be known to human understanding. It was a wise precaution, but it did not prevent the rise of millenarian movements in the late mediaeval ages, or the mutation of Christianity into the militant political religions of modern times.

In the thinkers of the Enlightenment who shaped the prevailing idea of progress, a Christian narrative of sin and redemption was joined with a Greek philosophy of liberation through knowledge. In Plato, this was an explicitly mystical philosophy, closely akin to those developed in India around the same time. For Hindus and Buddhists, history is a recurring dream; salvation is found in an awakening from time. In the secular faiths of the Enlightenment, this mystical gnosis becomes scientific knowledge; the aim is no longer wisdom, but control of the natural world. The message of all progressive creeds is that human emancipation comes from the growth of human power.

Today, outside a few atavistic sects, these creeds are dead. The stale hope of progress has no place in the creative life of the age. The paintings of Francis Bacon are the work of a godless Christian, the poetry of Ted Hughes of a true modern pagan. Contemporary humanism has yet to produce a single great artist. Yet – if only as an anodyne against intolerable anxiety – the idea of progress still pervades the culture. In the last analysis, it is an assertion of faith in human will – the most absurd faith of all.

History may have no meaning, it is often said, but 'we' can give it one. 'We' are not mankind, however; and the human animal is itself only a passing tremor in the life of the planet. The meaning believers in progress imagine they can impose on history is an expression of their own hopes and fears, and bound to be lost in the drift of time.

Fortunately, the Earth is larger and more enduring than anything produced by the human mind. For humans, the growth of knowledge means only history as usual – if on a rather larger scale of destruction. For the Earth, it is only a dream, soon to end in peace.

April 22, 2004

PART 1

THE ILLUSION OF PROGRESS

1

PROGRESS, THE MOTH-EATEN MUSICAL BROCADE

A great American poet, John Ashbery, wrote that tomorrow is easy, but today is uncharted. He put his finger on our real weakness. It is not our ignorance of the future which is incurable. It is our failure to understand the present.

Our view of the present time is overlaid with after-images from the recent past. At the moment, our idea of what it is to be modern is one of those after-images. We have inherited the faith that as the world becomes more modern it will become more reasonable, more enlightened and more balanced. We expect that, as modern habits of thinking advance across the world, people everywhere will become more like us – or at least as we imagine ourselves to be.

We think a truly modern world will be rational and forward-looking and that its values will be humane and cosmopolitan. We remain confident that the growth of scientific knowledge will allow us to control the risks of life and eliminate its worst evils – war, hunger and sickness.

Not all of this optimism is illusory. De Quincey's remark that a quarter of human suffering is toothache is worth remembering if ever we're tempted to think that little in the human lot can be improved. The contribution of anaesthetic dentistry to human well-being is a reminder that, in some fields, there have been unalloyed improvements, real progress. Even so, faith in progress is a superstition.

Nineteenth-century thinkers such as Karl Marx and John Stuart Mill believed that, as society and the economy become increasingly based on science, so our outlook on the world would become ever more rational. This is not to say that either man believed progress to be strictly inevitable; they did not rule out setbacks to the progress of reason. But what they never envisaged was that irrationality would continue to flourish alongside rapid advances in science and technology. The chief tenet of the Enlightenment is that the growth of knowledge is the key to human emancipation. No true believer in the Enlightenment would ever question that article of faith. Yet faith in progress through the growth of knowledge is itself irrational.

In fact, there is no consistent link between the adoption of modern science and technology on the one hand and the progress of reason in human affairs on the other. If anything, new technologies can give a new lease of life to the side of human nature that is not and will never be rational. The Taliban commander directing military operations from his cellular telephone is a familiar late twentieth-century figure. There is nothing in the spread of new technologies that regularly leads to the adoption of what we like to think of as a modern, rational worldview. Just as often, the result is fundamentalism.

This isn't a development confined to poor countries. In the United States, which sees itself as being at the cutting edge of modernity, political life is riven by religious conflicts. Neither America's continuing civil war over abortion, nor the attempt to drive Bill Clinton from office, can be understood unless we grasp that the world's most modern country is also one in which a fundamentalist minority can shape the political agenda. In Britain, the cult that surrounded the death of the Princess of Wales suggests that, while this country is certainly post-Christian, it has not become secular. Traditional religion is in retreat but it has not been replaced by rationality. Modern societies are full of occult and millenarian cults. They abound in new, short-lived religions, 'flickering and fading', as J G Ballard has put it, 'like off-peak commercials'.

With the nineteenth-century faith in progress we have inherited the belief that we can control the technologies we have invented and use them to advance human well-being. But think of the genetic technologies that are altering the food we eat and which make the cloning of human beings a realistic possibility. Some people see in these technologies the prospect of a great leap forward in which we shall defeat hunger and disease and eradicate disability. Others – and I am among these sceptics – welcome the potential benefits but fear that our new powers to remake nature and ourselves will be used in the service of hubristic fantasies. We can't renounce technology, and the idea that we can is just hubris in another guise. But we should recognize that, if we redesign nature to fit human wishes, we risk making it a mirror of our own pathologies. A world that has been rebuilt into a factory producing the things humans need or want will be a world without wilderness and from which many of the species with which we share the planet will disappear.

Who wants to live in such a world? What will human beings be like when they have been genetically re-engineered? And what will racists and tyrants do with the new power to remix human genes? If history is any guide, a world remade by genetic engineering may have a closer resemblance to H G Wells's *The Island of Dr Moreau* than to the dreams of today's technological utopians.

There is no power in the world that can ensure that technology is used only for benign purposes. Partly this is because we cannot agree on what such purposes are. Partly it is because even when enough people are agreed there is no power that can enforce the consensus. The institution on which we would have to rely for such enforcement – the modern state – is not up to the job.

In large parts of Africa, in much of Russia and some of its neighbours, in Colombia, Afghanistan, Pakistan and many other countries, the state has collapsed. In so far as anyone still has power in such countries, it has passed into the hands of tribal or religious militias, shadowy and fissiparous political organizations, criminal cartels or clans. The world today isn't a single political system any more than it is really a single economic system. It contains perhaps three or four dozen genuinely modern states with effective governments. Many other states are enfeebled or highly unstable; in large parts of the world, government has broken down and life has reverted to a pre-modern, semi-anarchic condition.

Economically the world is ruled by a sort of ramshackle laissez-faire. In a worldwide free market, corporations that try to exploit the commercial potential of genetically engineered crops will not be stopped by prohibition or tight regulation in one country or one group of countries such as the European Union. They will relocate to countries where such restraint is slight or non-existent. It is not difficult to do so when there is such a large choice of sovereign jurisdictions in the world and capital and production enjoy unfettered mobility between them.

The history of international efforts to stem the proliferation of weapons of mass destruction – nuclear, biological or whatever – offers little support for the hope that the spread of new technologies can be controlled. It is worth pondering how, even when the world's most powerful governments have an urgent and enduring interest in containing the spread of such weapons, their best efforts have succeeded only in slowing it down. It is hard enough to enforce nuclear non-proliferation agreements on a hundred or so fractious states. It is even harder to make them effective when, in many parts of the world, governments are no longer in charge.

Once a new technology is out in the world anyone can use it. At that point it becomes a weapon in human conflicts and an embodiment of human dreams. We are not masters of the tools we have invented. They affect our lives in ways we cannot control – and often cannot understand. The world today is a vast, unsupervised laboratory, in which a multitude of experiments are simultaneously under way.

Many of these experiments are not recognized as such. But the industrialization of agriculture, and the intensive use of fertilisers, pesticides and antibiotics to render plant and animal life unnaturally productive; the use and over-use of antibiotics in medicine; the widespread use of chemicals, illegal or prescribed, to alter mood or behaviour; mass air travel on the scale of the past 20 years or so – these and many other practices, which we have come to take for granted, are really experiments, carried out on a scale that defeats our understanding.

We can't know the risks of these experiments because we

don't understand their interactions with one another. We can't control our new technologies because we don't really grasp the totality of their effects. And there's a deeper reason why we are not masters of our technologies: they embody dreams of which we are not conscious and hopes that we cannot bear to give up. Late modern cultures are haunted by the dream that new technologies will conjure away the immemorial evils of human life.

But no new technology can abolish scarcity, do away with the necessity of choice or alter the fact of human mortality. For generations, techno-utopians have been telling us that tyranny would soon be obsolete. It is not so long since we were assured that television would make war impossible. Today there are those who believe that the virtual communities of the Internet will make dictatorship unworkable. There are even people who imagine that freezing our bodies or brains soon after the moment of our death could make us immortal.

Such techno-utopian fantasies deny some very obvious truths. New technologies strengthen repressive governments as well as weaken them. The rulers of China did not try to hush up the massacre in Tiananmen Square; they filmed it on video cameras and used it as a warning to others.

Similarly, the virtual communities of the Internet are powerless to overthrow tyranny. For that, the long haul of political struggle, with all its setbacks and sacrifices, is needed.

The idea that technology can do away with death encapsulates the most absurd denial of facts. Let's make the very large concession that preserving human bodies in a condition that allows them to be resuscitated is technically feasible. Even so, no technology that requires human bodies to be stored for generations or centuries is proof against war, changes in regime and the recurrent breakdowns of law and order that have occurred in every society of which we have knowledge.

For many, the promises of religion lack credibility; but the fear that inspires them has not gone away, and secular thinkers have turned to a belief in progress that is further removed from the basic facts of human life than any religious myth. When they look to technology to deliver us from accidents, from choice and even from mortality, they are asking from it something it cannot give: a deliverance from the conditions that make us human.

In his poem 'Aubade', Philip Larkin described religion as 'that vast moth-eaten musical brocade/created to pretend we never die'. Today the moth-eaten brocade is sewn from materials provided by science. Believers in progress are seeking from technology what they once looked for in political ideologies, and before that in religion: salvation from themselves.

April 9, 1999

2

BIOTECHNOLOGY AND THE POST-HUMAN FUTURE

Fidel Castro has ordered Cuban biotechnologists to clone a new breed of cow. The ageing *caudillo* sees the cloning project, which attempts to replicate White Udder, a cow that became legendary for its milk output in the 1980s, as a solution to Cuba's chronic shortage of dairy products. The benefits to Castro of resurrecting the animal, which died 17 years ago, extend well beyond its impact on the milk industry. A successful cloning would be a coup for Cuban biotechnology, a pointed reminder to the US that it is not always in the vanguard of scientific development, and a boost to the prestige of a crumbling regime.

The tangle of motives that has led Castro to become a cheerleader for biotechnology is a cautionary tale for anyone who imagines that the industry can be made subject to effective international regulation. In launching a scientific experiment for reasons that are at least partly political, Cuba's leader is doing what other countries have also done, and will surely do in the future. Such experiments are unlikely to be confined to non-human animals; within the lifetimes of people who are alive today, it will become feasible to alter human nature. If we believe what we are told by scientists, biotechnology offers more than the promise of removing genetic defects that contribute to common diseases: it opens up the possibility of redesigning human beings. The present generation will be able to shape the next in ways that have never before been possible. As scientific knowledge grows, it seems likely that not only the disease profiles, but also the personalities of future human beings will become alterable by human will. At that point, equipped with the new powers conferred by biotechnology, we will be what Lenin could only dream of becoming – engineers of souls.

It is a prospect that evokes both excitement and foreboding. Belatedly acknowledging that history may not have ended, Francis Fukuyama conjures up an intoxicating vision of a post-human future in which science enables us to reshape our very essence. But in his latest book (*Our Post Human Future: Consequences of the Biotechnology Revolution*) he warns that, as a result of un-even access to the new technologies, a genetic underclass could come into being, greatly magnifying existing inequalities. Worse, as envisioned in Aldous Huxley's *Brave New World*, a new underclass could be bred deliberately, reintroducing some-thing akin to slavery. These are real hazards; but, Fukuyama insists, they can be controlled by a well-constructed regime of regulation.

E O Wilson, on the other hand, while he acknowledges that the new technologies carry risks, argues that they open up a future of indefinite progress. In his books *Consilience: The Unity of Knowledge* and *The Future of Life*, Wilson declares that genetically modified crops can ease us through the environmental bottle-neck created by the expanding numbers of human beings. Beyond that, genetic engineering makes possible what he calls 'the conscious control of human evolution': a time when the

jerry-built structures of human nature have been recon-
structed, and humanity's development is no longer a matter of
blind evolutionary drift.

Wilson and Fukuyama thus differ in their assessment of the
comparative risks and benefits of the new technologies, but
where they are at one is in their belief that humanity can
master them. Here, they embody a paradox in contemporary
thinking. For both men, humans are best understood in
Darwinian terms of natural selection. Wilson, the greatest contemporary Darwinian and a genuinely profound thinker, is an
ardent foe of the myth of exemptionalism – the belief that
humans belong to a different order of things from the rest of
the natural world. In their origins and nature, he argues, they
are an animal species like any other. This is a conclusion that
Fukuyama, who has made wide-ranging (if at times ill-judged)
use of sociobiological theory, also accepts. Yet both thinkers
are adamant that humans can control their future development; and that, using scientific knowledge, they can overcome
the natural limits that frame the lives of other species.
Humanity can use the powers given by new technology to
bring about a world better than any that has ever existed.

This is faith, not science. By insisting that we can use our
powers of invention to control and direct our future, these
thinkers resurrect a religious image of humankind. According
to Christians, other animals may float along in the natural
drift of things, but humans can fashion their lives through
autonomous choices. That – and not merely its prodigious
inventiveness and awesome powers of destruction – is what
marks humanity off from the rest of life. This Christian idea
that humans are separated from other animals by an unbridge-
able gulf is not found in all, or even most religions. It is absent

from Hinduism and Buddhism, Taoism and Shinto. It is explicitly rejected in the primordial religion of mankind – animism – in which other animals figure on terms of equality with humans, if not superiority to them. Exemptionalism is a distinctively Christian doctrine. It is therefore not surprising that it should animate the political religions that have sprung up in the wake of Christianity's decline.

It is a commonplace that Marxism is a secular version of a Christian view of history, but the same is true of the vision of the human future that inspires thinkers such as Fukuyama and Wilson. Fukuyama's idea of the end of history makes sense only if history is a single continuous narrative, a moral drama involving all of humanity that concludes in some kind of universal completion. Once again, this is a peculiarly Christian view. No pagan thinker ever thought of history in this way. For Aristotle and the Roman historians, history is a series of cycles not unlike those found in the lives of plants. It has no purpose or end. Equally, Wilson's idea that humanity can take charge of its evolution makes sense only if you think humans are different in kind from every other animal species. In each case, these beliefs are inheritances from religion.

In *Our Posthuman Future*, Fukuyama announces 'the recommencement of history' on the grounds that science makes possible the transformation of human nature, and thereby new historical conflicts. The implication is that, were it not for scientific advance, his original pronouncement that history had ended would be vindicated. But this is to turn the role of science in history upside down; it is not science that drives history, but history that drives science. Pure scientists may have developed nuclear physics, but nuclear fission came into the world as a by-product of war. The same is true of many advances in radar technology, medicine and other fields. The urgent necessities of military conflict brought them into being, and economic forces determined their subsequent development. The new biotechnologies will be no different. In future, as in the past, the development of science and technology will be governed by war and profit.

This gives the lie to Fukuyama's repeated claim that, despite the destruction of the World Trade Center, his original pronouncement of the end of history still stands. As he now states it, his view is that liberal democracy offers the only legitimate regime anywhere in the world. Unlike his earlier, vaguer formulations, this at least has the intellectual merit of being false. Today, as in all previous times, regimes are legitimate to the extent that they meet vital human needs – needs such as security from violence, economic subsistence and the protection of cherished ways of life. There is nothing to say that the regimes that meet these needs must be democratic. The current regime in China derives its legitimacy from its capacity to guarantee order, promote prosperity and express the growing force of Chinese national identity. If it is challenged, it will be because it is failing to meet these needs, not because it fails to be democratic. To think that democratic values will ever be universally accepted is a basic error.

A similar fallacy infects Fukuyama's prognostications on biotechnology. He believes that an international consensus on the proper uses of genetic engineering can manage its hazards. Yet he says little about how a consensus can be enforced. The world contains nearly 200 sovereign states, many collapsed or heavily corroded by crime or corruption, others ruled by capricious tyrants, still others locked in bitter conflicts. How can we expect to regulate biotechnology when it has proved impossible to prevent the proliferation of weapons of mass destruction?

The military uses of biotechnology could pose a threat comparable to nuclear war. Genetically selective weapons may be developed – if they do not exist already – to target particular ethnic groups. Long-acting toxins may be devised that can devastate populations many years after being disseminated. Further ahead, reproductive cloning may be used to mass-manufacture soldiers more immune to emotions of sympathy and self-preservation than even today's suicide bombers. The development and spread of new weapons of mass destruction is a side effect of the growth of knowledge interacting with primordial human needs. That is why, finally, it is unstoppable. The same is true of genetic engineering. If people try, during the coming century, to redesign human beings, they will not do so on the basis of an enlightened international consensus. It will occur haphazardly, as part of competition and conflict among states, business corporations and criminal networks. The new, post-human creatures that may emerge from these murky rivalries will not be ideal types embodying the best human ideals: they will reproduce some of the worst features of unregenerate humanity.

When E O Wilson writes of humanity taking charge of its evolution, he enunciates the core belief of scientific humanism. Like other humanists, however, he has forgotten an important implication of Darwin's teachings: 'humanity' does not exist. The upshot of the theory of natural selection is that the human species is an accidental assemblage of genes, continuously mutating under the impact of changes in the environment. It is no more a collective entity capable of taking decisions about its future than any other animal species. Wilson's failure to grasp this truth gives his proposals for dealing with the environmental crisis an unmistakably utopian quality. He presents irrefutable evidence that human activity is wreaking great damage on the planet, and exterminating other living things at a rate unknown since the end of the dinosaurs. By his estimate, half the earth's plant and animal species will be gone by the end of the century. Yet, despite this overwhelming evidence of human fecklessness, Wilson insists that salvation can be found in science. Using new technologies, including genetically modified foods, the swelling human population can be fed. With population control and environmental conservation, the destruction of biodiversity can be arrested.

Wilson's programme is admirable; but it expresses a strangely unscientific, indeed irrational, faith in the human capacity for co-operation. If we look to history, we find no reason to think that science will ever be used to achieve a sustainable balance with the environment. On the contrary, the limits of growth are re-emerging as a major source of geostrategic conflict. As Wilson notes, since 1960, human numbers have doubled to around six billion. Barring catastrophes, they will rise by between two and four billion later this century. In the Gulf – a region entirely dependent on depleting supplies of oil for its income – the population will double in about 20 years. It does not take much insight into human behaviour to see that this is hardly a scenario for global co-operation. The combination of rising human numbers, dwindling natural resources and spreading weapons of mass destruction is more likely to unleash wars of unprecedented savagery. If we can bring ourselves to look clearly at this prospect, we will lay aside utopian fantasies of global co-operation. We will see our task as staving off disaster from day to day.

To account for the Fukuyama/Wilson faith that mankind can achieve conscious mastery of its evolution, we need to look back to an early nineteenth-century cult, French Positivism, which inspired not only Marx but also, through John Stuart Mill, many liberals, and it stands behind the faith in progress that is shared by all parties today.

Humanists believe their faith in progress is founded on reason, but it is not a result of scientific inquiry. It is the Christian idea of history as a universal narrative of salvation dressed up in secular clothes. Progressives believe that the growth of knowledge leads to the emancipation of humanity, but humans are highly inventive animals, who use their growing knowledge in the service of their most urgent needs – however conflicting, or ultimately self-destructive, these may prove to be. If the advance of reproductive cloning produces a new breed of post-humans, it will come about from the interplay of all-too-human forces and motives – war, profit and the vanity of leaders. The post-human future will not be the moment when humanity takes charge of its future, but one more blind turn in human history.

June 24, 2002

3

HOMO RAPIENS AND MASS EXTINCTION:
AN ERA OF SOLITUDE?

According to the Darwinian, Edward O Wilson, the earth is entering a new evolutionary era. We are on the brink of a great extinction the like of which has not been seen since the dinosaurs disappeared at the end of the Mesozoic Era, 65 million years ago. Species are vanishing at a rate of a hundred to a thousand times faster than they did before the arrival of humans. On current trends, our children will be practically alone in the world. As Wilson has put it, humanity is leaving the Cenozoic, the age of mammals, and entering the Eremozoic – the era of solitude.

The last mass extinction has not yet been fully explained. Many scientists believe it to have been the result of meteorites whose impact suddenly altered the global climate, but no one can be sure. In contrast, the cause of the current mass extinction is not in doubt: human expansion. As humans invade and exploit the last vestiges of wilderness, they destroy or destabilize the habitat of tens of thousands of species of plants, insects and animals. *Homo rapiens* is gutting the earth of biodiversity.

The lush natural world in which humans evolved is being

rapidly transformed into a largely prosthetic environment. Crucially, in any time-span that is humanly relevant, this loss of biodiversity is irreversible. True, life on earth recovered its richness after the last great extinction; but only after some ten million years had passed. Unless something occurs to disrupt the trends that are under way, all future generations of human beings will live in a world that is more impoverished biologically than it has been for aeons.

Given the magnitude of this change, one would expect it to be at the centre of public debate. In fact, it is very little discussed. Organizations such as the World Wildlife Fund press on with their invaluable work, and there are occasional reports of the destruction of wilderness; but for the most part, politics and media debates go on as if nothing is happening. There are many reasons for this peculiar state of affairs, including the ingrained human habit of denying danger until its impact is imminent; but the chief reason is that it has become fashionable to deny the reality of overpopulation.

In truth, the root cause of mass extinction is too many people. As Wilson puts : 'Population growth can justly be called the monster on the land.' Yet according to all the mainstream parties and most environmental organizations, the despoliation of the environment is mainly the result of flaws in human *institutions*. If we are entering a desolate world, the reason is not that humans have become too numerous; it is because injustice prevents proper use of the earth's resources. There is no such thing as overpopulation.

Interestingly, this view is not accepted in many of the world's poor countries. China, India, Egypt and Iran all have population programmes, as have many other developing nations. Opposition to population control is concentrated in rich parts of the world, notably the US, where the Bush administration pursues a fundamentalist vendetta against international agencies that provide family planning. It is under-standable that rich countries should reject the idea of overpopulation. In their use of resources, they are themselves the most overpopulated. Their affluence depends on their appropriating a hugely disproportionate share of the world's non-renewable resources. If they ever face up to that reality, they will have to admit that their affluence is unsustainable.

Another reason for denying the reality of overpopulation is that the growth in human numbers is extremely uneven. In some parts of the world, population is actually declining. This is strikingly true in post-communist Russia. A precipitate fall in public health and living standards has led to a virtually unprecedented population collapse, which is set to accelerate further as an African-style Aids die-off triggered by the coun-try's enormous numbers of intravenous drug users begins to take hold. In other countries, such as Japan, Italy and Spain, declining fertility is leading to zero or negative population growth. Such examples have given currency to the silly notion that overpopulation is no longer an issue – that, if anything, it is a slowdown in the growth of human numbers that we should be worrying about.

But while human numbers are falling in some parts of the world, in others they are exploding. Globally, the human popu-lation will continue to rise for at least a century – even if worldwide fertility falls to replacement level tomorrow. In 1940, there were around two billion humans on the planet. Today, there are about six billion. Even on conservative pro-jections, there will be nearly eight billion by 2050.

*

Eight billion people cannot be maintained without desolating the earth. Today, everyone aspires to live after the fashion of the world's affluent minority. That requires worldwide industrialization – as a result of which the human ecological footprint on the earth will be deeper than it has ever been.

Rainforests are the last great reservoirs of biodiversity, but they will have to be cleared and turned over to human settlement or food production. What is left of wilderness in the world will be made over to green desert. This is a bleak enough prospect, but what's worse is that it is a path from which there is no turning back. If a human population of this size is to be kept in existence, it must exploit the planet's dwindling resources ever more intensively. In effect, humans will turn the planet into an extension of themselves. When they look about the world, they will find nothing but their own detritus.

There are many who profess to be unfazed by this prospect. Marxists and free-market economists never tire of ridiculing the idea that other living things have intrinsic value. In their view, other species are just means to the satisfaction of human wants, and the earth itself is a site for the realization of human ambitions. These self-professed rationalists are prone to the conceit that theirs is a purely secular view of the world; but in thinking this way about the relationship of humans to the earth, they are in the grip of a religious dogma. The belief that the earth belongs to humans is a residue of theism. For Christians, humans are unique among animals because they alone are created in the image of God. For the same reason, they are uniquely valuable. It follows that humanity can behave as lord of creation, treating the earth's natural wealth and other animals as tools, mere instruments for the achievement of human purposes.

To my mind, such religious beliefs have caused an immense amount of harm, but at least they are coherent. It is perfectly reasonable to think humans are the only source of value in the scheme of things – so long as you retain the theological framework in which they are held to be categorically different from all other animals. But once you have given up theism, this sort of anthropocentrism makes no sense. Outside monotheistic religions, it is practically unknown. The view of things in which we are separate from the rest of nature and can live with minimal concern for the biosphere is not a conclusion of rational inquiry; it is an inheritance from a humanly aberrant religious tradition.

The fashionable belief that there is no such thing as over-population is part of an anthropocentric world-view that has nothing to do with science. At the same time, there is more than a hint of anthropocentrism in Wilson's suggestion that we are entering an age of solitude. The idea that, unlike any other animal, humans can take the planet into a new evolutionary era assumes that the earth will patiently submit to their inordinate demands. Yet there is already evidence that human activity is altering the balance of the global climate – and in ways that are unlikely to be comfortable for its human population. The long-term effects of global warming cannot be known with any certainty. But in a worst-case scenario that is being taken increasingly seriously, the greenhouse effect could wipe out densely populated coastal countries such as Bangladesh within the present century, while massively dislocating food production elsewhere in the world.

The result could be a disaster for billions of people. The idea that we are entering an era of solitude makes sense only if it is assumed that such a world would be stable, and hospitable to humans. Yet we know that the closer an eco-system comes to being a monoculture, the more fragile it becomes. The world's rainforests are part of the earth's self-regulatory system. As James Lovelock has observed, they sweat to keep us cool. With their disappearance, we will be increasingly at risk. A world overcrowded with humans that has been denuded of its biodiversity will be extremely fragile – far more vulnerable to large, destabilizing accidents than the complex biosphere we have inherited. Such a world is too delicate to last for long.

There are good reasons for thinking that an era of solitude will not come about at all. Lovelock has written that the human species is now so numerous that it constitutes a serious planetary malady. The earth is suffering from disseminated primatemaia – a plague of people. He sees four possible outcomes of the people plague: 'destruction of the invading disease organisms; chronic infection; destruction of the host; or symbiosis, a lasting relationship of mutual benefit to the host and the invader'.

The last two can be definitely ruled out. Humankind cannot destroy its planetary host. The earth is much older and stronger than humans will ever be. At the same time, humans will never initiate a relationship of mutually beneficial symbiosis with it. The advance of *Homo rapiens* has always gone with the destruction of other species and ecological devastation. Of the remaining outcomes, the second – in which over-numerous humans colonise the earth at the cost of weakening the biosphere – corresponds most closely to Wilson's bleak vision. But it is the first that is most likely. The present spike in human numbers will not last.

*

If it is not forestalled by changes in the planet's climate, we can be pretty sure that Wilson's era of solitude will be derailed by the side effects of human strife. Resource scarcity is already emerging as a factor aggravating tension in several regions of the world. In the coming century, it is set to be one of the primary causes of war. A world of eight billion people competing for vital necessities is highly unlikely to be at peace. On the contrary, it is programmed for endemic conflict. New technologies may blunt the edge of scarcity by allowing resources to be extracted and used more efficiently. But their key use will be to secure control over dwindling supplies of oil, natural gas, water and other essential inputs of industrial society.

The Internet originated in the military sector. Information technology is at the heart of the revolution in military affairs that is changing the face of war by powering the new generations of computer-guided missiles and unmanned planes. Only a couple of years ago, a host of air-headed publicists was proclaiming the arrival of a weightless world. The reality is just the opposite. The Gulf war was won with computers, and they will be critically important in any future war. In that sense, it is true that information technology will be the basis of prosperity in the twenty-first century. But its main contribution will not be to create a hypermodern, knowledge-driven economy; it will be to enable advanced industrial states to retain control of the most ancient sources of wealth – the world's shrinking supplies of non-renewable resources.

In the past, war has rarely resulted in a long-lasting decline in human numbers. But in a highly globalized world, it could have a new and more devastating impact. With a hugely increased population reliant on far-flung supply networks, large-scale war in the twenty-first century could do what it has frequently done in the past: trigger food shortages, even famine. Globalization no more engenders world peace than it guarantees an unending boom. It simply magnifies instability.

As we are now learning, globalization makes it harder to control the knock-on effects of stock market crashes. It may not be long before we learn that the same is true of war.

Summing up his view of the future, Wilson writes: 'At best, an environmental bottleneck is coming in the twenty-first century. It will cause the unfolding of a new kind of history driven by environmental change. Or perhaps an unfolding on a global scale of the old kind of history, which saw the collapse of regional civilizations, going back to the earliest in history, in northern Mesopotamia, and subsequently Egypt, then the Mayan and many others scattered across all the inhabited continents except Australia.'

Wilson's 'new kind of history' would involve a worldwide revolution in attitudes and policies. This would include universal access by women to the means of controlling their fertility, abandonment of the belief that there is a natural right to have as many children as you like, and a basic shift in attitudes to the environment in which it is accepted that our fate and that of the rest of life on earth are inseparably linked. These are the minimum conditions for Wilson's new kind of history.

Unfortunately, one has only to list these conditions to see that they are unrealisable. There cannot be a sustainable balance between natural resources and human needs so long as the number of people continues to increase, but a growing population can be seen as a weapon. Many Palestinians and Kurds view having large families as a survival strategy. In a world containing many intractable ethnic conflicts, there is unlikely to be a benign demographic transition to a lower birth rate.

The examples we have of societies in which population has declined in the absence of a big social crisis cannot be replicated worldwide. A policy of zero population growth requires universal availability of contraception and abortion, and limits on the freedom to breed; but the authority that could impose these conditions does not exist.

Homo rapiens has a long history of mass killing, but it has rarely chosen to regulate its numbers intelligently and humanely. If population declines, it will be as a result of war, genocide or the kind of generalized social collapse that has taken place in post-communist Russia.

The increase in human population that is currently under way is unprecedented and unsustainable. It cannot be projected into the future. More than likely, it will be cut short by the classical Malthusian forces of 'old history'. From a human point of view, this may be a discomforting prospect; but at least it dispels the nightmare of an age of solitude.

July 22, 2002

4

SEX, ATHEISM AND PIANO LEGS

Of all modern delusions, the idea that we live in a secular age is the furthest from reality. Throughout much of the world, religion is thriving with undiminished vitality. Where believers are in the minority, as they are in Britain today, traditional faiths have been replaced by liberal humanism, which is now established as the unthinking creed of thinking people. Yet liberal humanism is itself very obviously a religion – a shoddy replica of Christian faith markedly more irrational than the original article, and in recent times more harmful. If this is not recognized, it is because religion has been repressed from consciousness in the way that sexuality was repressed in Victorian times. Now, as then, the result is not that the need disappears, but rather that it returns in bizarre and perverse forms.

When thinking about the idea that we live in a secular era, it is worth remembering that the secular realm is itself a Christian invention. The biblical root of the secular state is the passage in the New Testament where Jesus tells his disciples to give to God what is God's and to Caesar what belongs to Caesar. Refined by Augustine and given a modern formulation with the Reformation, this early Christian commandment is the ultimate origin of the liberal attempt to separate religion from politics. In this, as in many other respects, liberalism is a neo-Christian cult.

Liberalism's religious roots are opaque to liberals today, but a little history makes them clear. In Britain, until the late nineteenth century, most liberals were believers. It was churchmen who most consistently upheld causes such as the abolition of slavery; the more radical thinkers belonged to fringe Christian denominations such as the Quakers and the Unitarians. Only with John Stuart Mill, influenced by the French Positivist Auguste Comte, did liberalism come to be closely associated with outright rejection of conventional religion.

Though Positivism is largely forgotten today, it was more influential than any other intellectual movement in shaping the humanist creed that has succeeded Christianity as the ready-made world-view of the British majority. The Positivists were not liberals – far from it. They aimed to found a new religion – the Religion of Humanity, as they called it – in which the human species would be worshipped as the supreme being, and they looked forward to a time when this new religion would have as much power as the Catholic Church had in mediaeval times. Eager to emulate the Church's rituals and hierarchies, they sought to replace the Catholic practice of crossing oneself by a secular version, in which positivist believers touched the bumps on their heads at the points where the science of phrenology had shown the impulses of order and benevolence to reside. They also installed a secular pope in Paris. In its early nineteenth-century heyday, the Positivist Church had Temples of Humanity in many parts of the world, including Britain. It was particularly successful in Latin

America, where a number of Positivist churches survive to this day.

The Positivist Church was a travesty, but its beliefs chimed with many of Mill's. Though he attacked Comte's anti-liberal tendencies, Mill did everything he could to propagate the Religion of Humanity. If he had some success, the reason was chiefly that the new humanist religion had a great deal in common with the creed it was meant to supplant. Liberal humanism inherits several key Christian beliefs – above all, the belief that humans are categorically different from all other animals. According to humanists, humans are unique in that, using the power over nature given them by science, they can create a world better than any that has existed before. In this view, the earth is simply a mass of resources for human use, and the other animals with which we share it have no value in themselves. Those who hold to this view of things see themselves as tough-minded scientific realists, but in fact they are in the grip of one of the worst legacies of Christianity.

The Positivist view of human possibilities had an enormous practical influence. Through its impact on Karl Marx, it inspired policies that resulted in environmental catastrophe in the former Soviet Union. The destruction of peasant farming and its replacement by agricultural collectives, which was foreshadowed in the writings of the founder of Positivism, Henri de Saint-Simon, led directly to the dust bowls and famines of the 1930s. The Positivist attempt to master nature was one of the causes of the downfall of the Soviet regime. Mikhail Gorbachev's commitment to a hubristic project of generating energy from dams created by flooding much of Siberia generated a far-reaching coalition of oppositional forces. Along with the aftershock of the nuclear meltdown at Chernobyl, those forces toppled the Soviet leader and the system he aimed to reform.

The role of hollowed-out versions of Christian myth in humanist thought is particularly clear in the case of Marxism. Marx's absurd idea of 'the end of history', in which communism triumphs and destructive conflict then vanishes from the world, is transparently a secular mutation of Christian apocalyptic beliefs. The same is true of Francis Fukuyama's equally absurd belief in universal salvation through 'global democratic capitalism'. In both cases, what we have is myth masquerading as science.

The trouble with secular myths is that they are frequently more harmful than the real thing. In traditional Christianity, the apocalyptic impulse was restrained by the insight that human beings are ineradicably flawed. In the secular religions that flowed from Christianity, this insight was lost. The result has been a form of tyranny, new in history, that commits vast crimes in the pursuit of heaven on earth.

The role of humanist thought in shaping the past century's worst regimes is easily demonstrable, but it is passed over, or denied, by those who harp on about the crimes of religion. Yet the mass murders of the twentieth century were not perpetrated by some latter-day version of the Spanish Inquisition. They were carried out by atheist regimes in the service of Enlightenment ideals of progress. Stalin and Mao were not believers in original sin. Even Hitler, who despised Enlightenment values of equality and freedom, shared the Enlightenment faith that a new world could be created by human will. Each of these tyrants imagined that the human condition could be transformed through the use of science.

History has demolished these ambitions. Even so, they have not been abandoned. In dilute and timorous forms, they continue to animate liberal humanists. Humanists angrily deny harbouring the vast hopes of Marx or Comte, but still insist that the growth of scientific knowledge enables mankind to construct a future better than anything in the past. There is not the slightest scientific warrant for this belief. It is faith, pure and simple. More, it is Christian faith – the myth that, unlike other animals, 'we' can shape the future.

It is a commonplace that science has displaced religion. What is less often noted is that science has become a vehicle for needs that are indisputably religious. Like religion in the past, though less effectively, science offers meaning and hope. In politics, improvement is fragmentary and reversible; in science, the growth of knowledge is cumulative and now seemingly unstoppable. Science gives a sensation of progress that politics cannot deliver. It is an illusion, but that in no way diminishes its power. We may live in a post-Christian culture, but the idea of providence has not disappeared; people still need to believe that a benign pattern can be glimpsed in the chaos of events.

The need for religion appears to be hard-wired in the human animal. Certainly the behaviour of secular humanists supports this hypothesis. Atheists are usually just as ardently engaged as believers. Quite commonly, they are more intellectually rigid. One cannot engage in dialogue with religious thinkers in Britain today without quickly discovering that they are, on the whole, more intelligent, better educated and strikingly more freethinking than unbelievers (as evangelical atheists still incongruously describe themselves). No doubt there are many reasons for this state of affairs, but I suspect it is the repression of the religious impulse that explains the obsessive rigidity of secular thought.

Liberal humanists repress religious experience – in themselves and others – in much the same way that sexuality was repressed in the strait-laced societies of the past. When I refer to repression here, I mean it in precisely the Freudian sense. In secular cultures, religion is buried in the unconscious, only to reappear – as sex did among the Victorians – in grotesque and illicit forms. If, as some claim, the Victorians covered piano legs in a vain effort to exorcise sex from their lives, secular humanists behave similarly when they condemn religion as irrational. It seems not to have occurred to them to ask where it comes from. History and anthropology show it to be a species-wide phenomenon. There is no more reason to think that we will cease to be religious animals than there is to think we will some day be asexual.

Whatever their disciples may say today, Karl Marx and John Stuart Mill were adamant that religion would die out with the advance of science. That has not come about, and there is not the remotest prospect of it happening in the foreseeable future. Yet the idea that religion can be eradicated from human life remains an article of faith among humanists. As secular ideology is dumped throughout the world, they are left disoriented and gawping.

It is this painful cognitive dissonance, I believe, that accounts for the peculiar rancour and intolerance of many secular thinkers. Unable to account for the irrepressible vitality of religion, they can react only with puritanical horror and stigmatize it as irrational. Yet the truth is that if religion is irrational, so is the human animal. As is shown by the behaviour of humanists, this is never more so than when it imagines itself to be ruled by reason.

The result of repressing religious needs has been a rash of secular cults. Among these, liberal humanism – the successor of Comte's Religion of Humanity – has been the most successful. This is partly because it is so closely modelled on Christianity, but also because it has been able to claim the authority of science. In fact, though it contains some fairly well established theories (such as Darwinism), science cannot yield a fixed world-view of the sort offered by religion. It is essentially provisional. Nor can it offer a substitute for religious hopes. In the minds of humanists, scientific advance is linked with progress in ethics and politics; but they can think this way only because they have taken the precaution of forgetting the past. The evidence of history is that scientific knowledge is used to further the goals that people already have. The idea that society advances in tandem with science is simply a myth.

Here we have the paradox of secularism. Secular societies believe they have left religion behind, when all they have done is substitute one set of myths for another. It is far from clear that this amounts to an improvement. Christian myth has harmful aspects, not least its ingrained anthropocentrism. Even so, in insisting that human nature is incorrigibly flawed it is far more realistic than the secular doctrines that followed it. In effect, liberal humanism has taken Christianity's unhappiest myth – the separation of humans from the rest of the natural world – and stripped it of the transcendental content that gave it meaning. In so doing, it has left secular cultures such as Britain stuck between a humanist view of mankind that actually comes from religion and a more genuinely scientific view in which it is just one animal species, no more capable of taking charge of its destiny than any other.

As we know it in Britain today, the secular world-view is simply the Christian view of the world with God left out. Liberal humanism is the contemporary version of an eccentric nineteenth-century cult – less colourful than its Positivist precursor, no doubt, but just as clearly modelled on Christianity. Religious thinkers understand this and look forward to a post-secular age. Befogged missionaries for a dull Victorian heresy, secular thinkers remain stuck in the past.

Humanism is not an alternative to religious belief, but rather a degenerate and unwitting version of it. Among the many varieties of religious life that are thriving among us – Hindu and Buddhist, Jewish and Muslim, along with many new and hybrid traditions – this pale shadow of Christianity is an anachronism.

Weighed down with fears and anxieties that the rest of us have never known or have long since left behind, it survives only as a remnant of a time when religion suppressed natural human impulses. We may not be far from a time when atheism will be seen as a relic of repression, like the frills that may once have been draped over piano legs.

December 16, 2002

5

FAITH IN THE MATRIX

In the film *The Matrix* a character called Agent Smith asks: 'Did you know that the First Matrix was designed to be a perfect human world, where none suffered, where everyone would be happy? It was a disaster.' A computer-generated virtual environment, the Matrix is a system designed to control humans. The inhabitants of this hallucinatory world take it to be real; they imagine themselves working and playing, making war and having sex, living normal human lives. In reality, they are floating in pod-like vats hooked up to the machine, their experiences induced in them by the program that runs the computer.

The Matrix (1999) and *The Matrix Reloaded* (2003) are densely allusive action movies, in which fantastical martial arts scenes are intermixed with cryptic dialogue and a labyrinthine plot. Designed and marketed to manufacture a cult, they have succeeded in generating a thriving industry of interpreters. Philosophers have wheeled their rusty devices on to the set and used them to view the films as exercises in scepticism about the external world. More interestingly and plausibly, scholars of religion have analysed the films in mythic terms, finding traces of Christianity, Buddhism and Gnosticism. With a media product of this kind there is no deep meaning waiting to be deciphered, and it is silly to claim exclusive validity for any interpretation; but the films have a definite political resonance, suggesting a sardonic and uncomfortable commentary on the way our world is ruled.

They show humans as prisoners of the machine, 'batteries' that it drains for energy while keeping them entranced and powerless. Such images are easily read as banal signifiers for capitalist exploitation, but a more intriguing reading is suggested by Agent Smith's allusion to the First Matrix. The goal of that programme was not exploitation; it was to design a perfect world. The consequent disaster is not specified, but the films suggest that the unreal world of the Matrix is the outcome of an attempt to redesign the real world so that it no longer contains suffering and evil. In the past, religion was the vehicle for such fantasies; in more recent times they were expressed in utopian political projects, such as communism and neo-liberalism. Whereas the great religions wisely promise an end to evil and suffering only in the hereafter, these utopian cults aimed to achieve the same goal here on earth.

Today, faith in political action is practically dead, and it is technology that expresses the dream of a transformed world. Few people any longer look forward to a world in which hunger and poverty are eradicated by a better distribution of the wealth that already exists. Instead, governments look to science to create ever more wealth. Intensive agriculture and genetically modified crops will feed the hungry; economic growth will reduce and eventually remove poverty. Though it is often politicians who espouse these policies most vociferously, the clear implication of such technical fixes is that we might as well forget about political change. Rather than struggling against arbitrary power, we should wait for the benign effects of growing prosperity.

It may well be true that we cannot cure the worst evils by political action: if an absurdity like the Iraq war cannot be prevented, what hope is there of governments eradicating hunger? Yet technology is not a surrogate for political action. In practice, we simply use it to mask problems we cannot solve.

As traditional forms of social control are swept away, we turn to pervasive video surveillance to stop crime. As terrorism grows, we deploy smart bombs against 'rogue states'. We use Prozac and similar drugs not only to cope with episodes of depression, but increasingly to suppress normal human responses of frustration and disappointment. New media technologies enable us to blank out the environments in which we live. Plugged into our Walkman, we can forget the squalor by which we are actually surrounded.

Even when we are not insulated in this way, our view of the world is deformed by the mass media. Each day, we may encounter a filthy environment and dysfunctional public services, but in the virtual world conjured up by interactive television we are all only a moment away from wealth and freedom. For many people, this fantasy world is more real than their disjointed everyday actions and perceptions. The Matrix shows the logical outcome: a dream-filled half-life passed in a simulated environment. A degenerate product of the human longing for a better world, the Matrix is the ultimate technology of escape.

The idea of a technology that can create virtual worlds is usually attributed to American computer scientists, who began writing about virtual reality in the 1980s and 1990s. But the Polish science fiction writer Stanislaw Lem anticipated it some decades earlier. In his *Summa Technologiae*, published in 1964, Lem envisaged a Phantomat, a virtual reality machine that allows its users to exit the real world and enter a simulated environment of their own choosing. In the real world we are delicate organisms that can only live once, but in the Phantomat we can live over and over again as whatever we want to be. The Phantomat gives us what mystics have always sought – liberation from the material world. Rid of our mortal bodies, we can roam cyberspace for all eternity.

But, Lem believed, the more realistic the virtual world the machine creates, the more imprisoned we are in our own imaginations. As our embodied selves, we interact with a world we know only in part, and which operates independently of our desires. In contrast, the virtual worlds we encounter in the Phantomat are human constructions. Fabricated from our dreams, they are worlds in which nothing can be hurt or destroyed because nothing really exists. In short, they are worlds in which nothing really matters.

Lem feared that humanity might come to prefer the virtual worlds of the Phantomat. It is a fear echoed in *The Matrix*, when a character called Cypher chooses a life of pleasure and illusion over the contingencies of life outside the programme. He is happy to defend his choice. 'You know, I know this steak doesn't exist. I know that when I put it into my mouth, the Matrix is telling my brain that it is juicy and delicious . . . you know what I realize?' He takes a bite of steak. 'Ignorance is bliss.'

Lem's suspicion that humanity might opt for the dream world of the Phantomat over the intractable conflicts of the real world is well founded. Much of the affluent majority in western countries make the same choice as Cypher. They opt to live in the virtual world created by the mass media, knowing full well that it is an illusion. Here I mean not just 'reality television', which conjures up a world from which commuting, debt, illness and almost all the activities in which we actually pass our days have been banished. Look at media reportage of war. We know that bereavement, mutilation and unhealed psychological scars linger on for generations after wars have officially ended; but we do not want to be unnecessarily reminded of these things. We honour the reporters who insist on reporting the aftermath of war, but we are secretly relieved when the media move on. That way, we can avoid the pain of too much reality and sustain the virtual world we prefer to inhabit.

It is in no way far-fetched, then, to think that many people might opt for an unreal life in the Phantomat. Even so, Lem's fear that humanity might exit the actual world for an eternal half-life in cyberspace is groundless. The virtual environments that may be possible in future through the use of ever more advanced computer programs may be more realistic than anything that we can now create or even imagine; but they will never enable humanity to detach itself completely from the earth. No computer will ever create a self-sustaining virtual world. The dream of humanity spending eternity in cyberspace is just a nightmare.

There are several reasons why virtual reality machines will always fail in the end. For one thing, all virtual environments have a definite material basis. In the hallucinatory kung fu scenes that are interspersed throughout *The Matrix*, nothing seems impossible: the human figures that enact these brilliantly choreographed stunts are infinitely reproducible simulacra, not finite vulnerable organisms. Yet the Matrix itself is finally a finite material thing, a programme encrypted in a tangle of wires and plastic; it is vulnerable to decay and accident. As a result, the virtual environment fabricated in the Matrix will not renew itself indefinitely. Sooner or later, it will be corroded by time and chance. Anomalies will creep into the program, and the Matrix will be infected with flaws. The perfect virtual world will be perfect no longer. It will plainly be revealed as what it had never ceased to be – a fragile construction perilously situated in the unstable material world.

And like the Phantomat, the Matrix is a human invention. Even if they are devised by an artificial intelligence that has evolved far beyond humanity, these simulated worlds are ultimately by-products of human knowledge. They cannot escape the finitude and imperfection that go with their animal origins. They will inescapably contain errors and distortions. The picture of the world we have as humans is a makeshift that has evolved to help us in the animal struggle for survival. We can be certain it contains errors we will never discover.

Perhaps the artificial intelligences we invent will evolve to overcome these built-in flaws but, if they do, they will only develop errors of their own, which will infect any virtual worlds they create. However devised, any virtual reality machine will contain traces of its earthly genesis, which are bound to disrupt the perfection of the virtual world. It is these ineradicable imperfections that make Lem's vision of perfect unreality itself unrealistic.

On some interpretations, there is another source of disruption in the virtual world of the Matrix – human free will. The inhabitants of the Matrix are entranced; but once they become aware that they are living in a dream world, they can rebel.

This is an initially plausible reading – much of the films' plots have to do with possibilities of revolt – but it does not make much sense. Recall that Cypher willingly opts for a life of unreality. He is not being controlled when he tucks into his virtual steak; he knows the steak is an illusion, but enjoys it all the same. Cypher has not so much given up his freedom as exercised it in order to live a lie.

If viewing the films as fables of revolt against tyranny is not apt, it is just as wrong to see them as addressing free will in a metaphysical sense. Set aside philosophical disputation about what free will might mean, and whether we have it. However the tiresome old conundrum is settled, freedom of will is not something we can lose as a result of a new technology. If humans possess it at all they cannot be deprived of it in the Matrix: they may be reduced to a state of passivity, but they will still remain agents capable of determining their own course of action. That much is clear, but it would be a pity if the meaning of these fascinating films were reduced to so dull and obvious a thought.

Falling back on hoary debates about free will or conventional notions about the value of freedom does not yield an interpretation that does justice to these films. In a curious, oblique way these are political films, but the questions they suggest are not hackneyed ones about capitalist exploitation or media tyranny. They are about the affluent majority colluding with the media in sustaining an unreal view of the world. More deeply, they suggest that the view of things propagated by the media cannot be other than unreal. Today, nearly everyone believes that technology can remake the world. If only invention is allowed to flourish, hunger will be eradicated, poverty will disappear and tyranny will no longer be a temptation.

It is the emptiness of these hopes that condemns the media to propagating fantasies. There is no market for the truth that many of our problems are actually insoluble. Whereas religion once enabled us to tolerate this awkward fact, today it has become almost unmentionable. Driven from politics by repeated disaster, the dream of perfection has moved on to technology. The Matrix films are amazing feats of technical wizardry. If they contain a message, however, it is that technology is not magic. It cannot alter the facts of human life.

June 23, 2003

6

WHEN THE MACHINE STOPS

The crowds milling gently around Charing Cross Station when the power failed did not look too worried. Many seemed to view the breakdown as nothing out of the ordinary – just another trial in the daily ordeal of commuting. A few, perhaps welcoming the sudden disruption of their daily routine, made off for nearby coffee shops and bookstores when it became clear that normal service would not be resumed any time soon. Some were heard muttering about the outage that had blacked out New York and much of the eastern coast of North America, but nobody panicked.

The unruffled confidence I observed on the night of the outage continued in its aftermath. Experts on the National Grid described the power failure as a 'unique event', well beyond the reach of any kind of contingency planning. Others hinted that it might be the shape of things to come. Either way, we needn't worry. This was a glitch, perhaps of a kind to which we would have to accustom ourselves in future, but certainly not a crisis.

The consensus is that there is nothing in such events to suggest that our way of life is threatened. We have come to think of our rich, energy-intensive societies as normal, and we cannot take seriously the possibility that they may be unsustainable. Even when we are confronted with evidence that our high-tech way of life is fragile, we insist that this is not a fundamental flaw, but merely a technical problem.

Starting in Britain less than 250 years ago, industrialization has swept the world, and along with it has gone increased longevity and higher living standards. Why shouldn't this growth go on indefinitely? If there are problems, they can be overcome. There seems to be no reason why our present way of life should not last indefinitely and spread to all of humanity.

The belief that our way of life can be replicated across the world is accepted by just about everybody. It is an integral part of the faith in progress that has replaced religion in most of the advanced industrial societies, and the basis of development programmes throughout the world. Yet it is a dream no more realizable than the fantasies of the early nineteenth-century utopian socialist Charles Fourier, who has been forever mocked for believing that the oceans would some day be composed of lemonade.

We have had it drummed into our heads that utopian thinking has a natural home on the left, but today it is found right across the political spectrum. All parties subscribe to the faith that there are no limits on human ambition that cannot be overcome with technology. The recent outages are seen as technical failures. Privatization, it is said, may have made energy infrastructures more vulnerable, but there is nothing wrong with them that cannot be fixed.

The unprecedented recent power failures reveal a deeper truth. Human ambitions may be limitless, but the earth's resources are irrevocably finite. Our present way of life cannot renew itself without cheap energy; but the resources from which energy is extracted are becoming inexorably scarcer and more expensive. At the same time, they are becoming a focus of conflict between states.

As countries such as Britain and the US become ever more dependent on energy originating in faraway regions, they are drawn increasingly into trying to secure control of them by military means. Conflict in the Middle East has an extremely complex history, but anyone who tells you that western intervention in the region has nothing to do with oil is a fool or a liar. In central Asia, the Great Game has been resumed, with the major powers vying for access to the region's reserves of oil and natural gas. Behind all the rhetoric about humanitarian intervention, the hard realities of classical geopolitics have returned.

The social theories we have inherited from the nineteenth century tell us that industrialization enables scarcity in the necessities of life to be abolished. Karl Marx and Herbert Spencer may not have agreed about many things, but they shared an unshakeable faith that industrialism could rid humanity of the worst forms of material deprivation – and thereby of the wars of scarcity that had plagued it in the past. Worldwide industrialization would put an end to the savage competition for resources that dominates much of human history.

This fanciful nineteenth-century creed is now the basis of mainstream economics. For most economists, there is no such thing as scarcity, only price. If there is growing demand for natural resources, they will become more expensive. New resources will be found, or new technologies developed, and economic growth will continue. In this view, there is no reason why a dwindling natural resource should spark military conflict. Market pricing and technological innovation can be relied upon – at least over the long run – to overcome any shortage that may temporarily arise.

In the 1990s, this eccentric creed was repackaged and sold to governments. Given a spurious rigour by economists, it became the intellectual basis for the global free market. Yet its influence over policy has never extended to defence planning. Bien-pensant economists can babble on as much as they like about the pacifying effects of free markets, but military strategists continue to take for granted that secure access to energy sources is a strategic imperative. Advanced industrial societies would collapse if they were cut off from them for more than a few months. No new technology can prevent such a disaster.

Talk of new sources of energy replacing oil in the long run is all very well, but history is one short run after another. The first Gulf war was waged to protect western oil supplies, and for no other reason. Iraq's vast oil reserves are not the only reason that country was invaded, but they are a vitally important factor. If, as some strategists believe is likely, military conflict breaks out between China and the United States over the next few decades, it will be partly because they are the chief competitors for the world's shrinking reserves of cheap oil. The rising demand for energy has become a cause of war.

Contrary to the theories of progress bequeathed to us from the nineteenth century, worldwide industrialization is not banishing scarcity in the necessities of existence and ushering in a new era of peace. It is creating new scarcities and triggering new conflicts. Without oil, the energy-intensive agriculture on which we rely so heavily could not exist. A steady supply of oil is as important in our lives as good weather was in the agrarian societies of the past.

As reserves are depleted, we become dependent on lines of supply that cross highly unstable regions of the world. With North Sea oil production peaking, a growing proportion of Britain's energy will originate in central Asia, coming via long pipelines. Along the way, it will be vulnerable to every kind of political risk, including terrorism.

Our present way of life is more prone to disruption than most people think, and its fragility is increasing. We tend to think that as global networks widen and deepen, the world will become a safer place, but in many contexts the opposite is true. As human beings become closely interlinked, breakdowns in one part of the world spread more readily to the rest. The so-called 'millennium bug' never materialized, but the extreme delicacy of the virtual ties that bind us together is demonstrated in recurrent computer viruses. It is probably only a matter of time before cyber-terrorists disable power stations and airports by hacking into their computer control systems.

In global financial markets, the instantaneous transmission of information was supposed to engender stability. In fact, it has produced enormous movements of speculative capital, often triggered by computer programs, that can threaten the entire financial system. The meltdown in 1998 of Long-Term Capital Management – a hedge fund advised by Nobel Prize-winning economists – shows that systemic risk of this kind is not a fantasy of doom-mongers.

What is truly fantastical is the notion that global economic expansion can continue indefinitely. Exponential growth cannot go on forever, and we may already be reaching its limits. In so far as it is humanly caused, global warming is a by-product of advancing industrialization. As more human beings adopt an energy-intensive way of life, climate change can only accelerate. The profligate lifestyle of a few rich countries cannot be sustained, still less exported worldwide. The earth itself stands in the way.

Nothing infuriates true believers in progress as much as the observation that the planet imposes insuperable limits on their ambitions. Human intelligence can transform the planet, they insist, and create a future for humanity better than anything it has known in the past. A utopian faith in the power of tech-nology runs right through modern western thought, and it is found in the unlikeliest of places. Centrist politicians who believe that globalization cannot be stopped take for granted that it will not be derailed by ecological crisis or war. Yet in the longer sweep of history, that is exactly how many civilizations have ended. Why should ours be any different?

Green thinkers believe that our current economic system can be radically reformed and thereby made more sustainable, but they fail to take the full measure of the difficulties that lie ahead. In time, worldwide industrialization will be cut short by ecological crisis, but it is impossible to stop it or slow it down by political means. Nor is it clearly desirable to attempt to do so. Human numbers are already too high for any reversion to localized economies to be feasible, and they will rise substan-tially over the coming half-century. Much more can be done in developing technologies that are environment-friendly, but an economy based on solar energy and wind power cannot sup-port eight billion people.

Where greens are right is in thinking that a fundamental

shift in the way we live is inevitable. Conventional thinkers of all stripes think in terms of increasing global interdependence, but the more closely integrated the world becomes, the more vulnerable it is to destabilizing shocks. A Rousseauesque world of small agrarian communities does not figure in any realistic scenario – fortunately, in my view – but a more fragmented world could be more humanly sustainable than the one we live in today.

There is an ingrained tendency to think of progress in terms of convergence on a global way of life and, up to a point, a global viewpoint is unavoidable. Pollution and climate change do not respect borders, and war or anarchy in any part of the world has spill-over effects on the rest, but we should discard the idea that one sort of regime is best for everybody. Instead of thinking of progress as a movement towards a single, ideal way of life, we could think of it in terms of different ways of life developing in their own ways. If some countries wish to opt out of the global market, they should be free to do so. If they want to pick and choose among new technologies, let them try.

A world in which different ways of life coexist in peace is an attractive prospect, but it is infinitely remote from the trajectory of events. As we look ahead, a less tightly integrated world seems inescapable, but it will come into being through a piecemeal and at times extremely painful adjustment to the fragility of the high-tech lifestyle we have adopted. When a more balanced world eventually emerges, it will be after many crises, and after our present utopian faith in technology has been consigned to the rubbish heap of history.

September 8, 2003

7

SCIENCE AS A VEHICLE FOR MYTH

Recalling a congress of communist writers that he attended in the 1930s, Arthur Koestler described how a simple question reduced the meeting to silence. Bored beyond endurance by the eulogies to the new world that would come into being once scientific socialism had been installed, André Malraux asked impatiently: 'And what about the man who is run over by the tramcar?' There was an awkward pause – but not for long. Soon a right-thinking comrade supplied the answer: 'In a perfect socialist transport system, there will be no accidents.'

Koestler's story contains a forbidden truth. The great projects of human emancipation that shaped the past century claimed to be based on science, but they were actually founded on myths. In holding out the prospect of a world without senseless accidents, communism renewed the eschatological hopes of western religion. History might seem a mix of drift and disaster, but it unfolds under divine guidance; a day will come when no one dies in vain. In the past, it was believed that God would bring about this happy state. Revolutionary movements such as communism promised something even more miraculous. By using the power of science, human beings could create it themselves.

Science is supposed to be the pursuit of truth, but in secular cultures it has become the chief vehicle for myth. The human needs that were once expressed in religion have not disappeared. From the cult of cryogenics to absurd neo-Darwinian ideas, the core myths of western religion are being recycled as science. In the course of this transformation, the wisdom they contain is being lost. Growing scientific knowledge is not producing a more rational view of the world, but a secular mythology that is further from the truth of the human condition than the religious myths of the past.

Communism proved to be a mirage. Millions of people died in the search for a non-existent earthly paradise, but that has not stopped the search. Towards the end of the twentieth century neo-liberals peddled a version of the same myth. Global capitalism would do what communism had failed to do – bring freedom and prosperity to all of humankind. Though it began on the Right, the cult of the free market was like communism in being a revolutionary creed. Just like Marx and Engels in the Communist Manifesto, neo-liberals believed that they had solved the riddle of history.

Both Marxists and neo-liberals insist that their promises of a radiant future are the result of rigorous scientific inquiry, but their adamant conviction betrays the true source of their beliefs. Marxism and neo-liberalism are ersatz religions in which the Christian myth of the end of history is rendered into the idiom of science. Missionaries of central planning may quarrel with votaries of the free market about which is the best economic system, but they are at one in their belief that, once it has been adopted, worldwide prosperity and universal peace will inevitably follow.

In fact, at the start of the twenty-first century, Marxism and neo-liberalism are discredited creeds. Ageing Trotskyists may even now be gathering in their cells to plot the coming revolution and pious free-marketeers huddled together in listless seminars on the glories of global capitalism, but the faith in salvation through politics is dead. If communism was a tragedy, neo-liberalism has been a farce. After all the babble about the irresistible spread of democracy and free markets, the reality is war, protectionism and the shifty politics of secrecy and corruption – in other words, history as usual. Outside the Trotskyist sects and the right-wing think-tanks, no one believes that the world can be remade by revolutionary politics. The fantasy may linger on in the anti-globalization movement, but even there it is more an expression of fear of the future than a genuine conviction.

Yet eschatological myths have not disappeared, only shifted into other areas. In his seminal study *The Pursuit of the Millennium* (originally published in 1957), Norman Cohn showed that modern revolutionary movements were animated by beliefs in many ways similar to those of millenarian movements in late-medieval Europe. Both saw history in apocalyptic terms: the old world was coming to an end and a new world being born. Today, secular cultures are looking to science for salvation. Politics has been replaced by technology as the focus of eschatological hope.

A curious example of the fusion of eschatology and technology is the Californian cryogenics movement. Followers of this cult have themselves frozen – or sometimes just their heads, if they cannot afford the whole deal – in the faith that, with the progress of science, it will one day be possible to bring them back from the dead. There has been some dispute about the scientific credentials of this process and doubts have been raised regarding the probity of some of the companies providing it, but these are details. The point is that what is on offer is a technological surrogate for immortality. Just as Christianity promises the resurrection of the body, cryogenics offers the prospect of never having to die – but whereas the Christian promise is accepted on faith, that of cryogenics is supposed to be based on science. In fact, it is far more incredible than any of the promises of religion.

The main trouble with seeking immortality through technology is not that the technology does not exist. Maybe some day it will – but even if techniques are developed for defrosting frozen cadavers and returning them to some semblance of life, these new technologies will not grant immortality. Believers in technological immortality assume that the laws and institutions that exist now will last indefinitely, but in doing so they are taking for granted a degree of economic and political stability that has no precedent. In effect, the possibility of cryonic resurrection depends on the belief that the society we have today is immortal.

Developing the new technologies may take hundreds of years, but over such a time-span there are bound to be large-scale discontinuities in law and politics. If the companies that store the waiting cadavers do not go under in stock market crashes, they will be swept away by war or revolution. These may seem apocalyptic possibilities, but they are only history carrying on as it has always done. What is truly apocalyptic is the belief that history will come to a stop.

Seeking perpetual life through cryogenics is a fringe pursuit, but it illustrates a more widespread phenomenon. Science has not done away with myth. It has enabled the myths of the past to survive in new forms. There is nothing in science that points to immortality as a realistic possibility for humans. The lesson of science is that death has a vital function in the natural environment. In the only world we know, nothing is immortal. The hope of escaping death comes from religion, not science. Yet science has given this mystical hope a new lease on life.

A striking example is the way in which Darwinism has been used to bolster belief in progress. Darwin's theory says nothing about whether the results of natural selection are good or bad. It simply describes a biological mechanism at work. So far as Darwinism is concerned, the world has no built-in tendency to improvement. The natural selection of genetic mutations may lead to more complex life forms, but equally it may wipe them out. This is much too austere a vision ever to be popular. The hopes bequeathed by Christianity are too deep and pervasive in the culture for such a vision of purposeless change to be accepted. As a result, Darwin's theory has been turned upside down and used to prop up prevailing notions of progress.

The most familiar examples are varieties of social Darwinism. In the late nineteenth century, erroneous versions of evolutionary theory were used to give support to laissez-faire capitalism and European imperialism. In the late twentieth century, a form of social Darwinism was revived on the American right to give a spurious explanation of the country's stark racial inequalities. These are pretty crude uses of science for political ends. Not only is the science shoddy, so are the ends that are being pursued. More interesting are recent attempts to use Darwinism to give the idea of human progress a scientific basis.

Richard Dawkins's theory of memes is a neo-Darwinian account of the spread of ideas. As Dawkins makes clear in his book *The Selfish Gene* (1976), memes include tunes and catch-phrases, ways of making pots or building arches, political ideas and scientific theories. Dawkins's theory is that just as genes propagate themselves by moving from body to body via spermatozoa or eggs, so memes propagate themselves by moving from brain to brain. Actually, it is unclear whether this is really a theory or simply a rather inept analogy, for though he talks loosely of the propagation of memes occurring by a process of imitation, Dawkins never specifies a definite mechanism for the transmission of ideas. Nor is this surprising, given that no such mechanism exists.

It has long been known that ideas can spread by a kind of contagion, but in the history of ideas there is nothing resembling the natural selection of genetic mutations in biology. Persecution and war, the power of wealth and the ability of governments to shape the news are only some of the factors explaining why some ideas spread and others do not. Imitation may have a part in this complicated process, but it can hardly be said to explain it.

Even if the spread of ideas could be explained by some simple mechanism akin to natural selection, it would in no way ensure that good ideas prevailed. The worst ideas are often the most efficient in propagating themselves. Take anti-Semitism, one of the most poisonous memes in history and one of the most successful. Or consider the religious beliefs against which Dawkins rails with evangelical passion. As he himself admits, ideas such as eternal damnation have an awesome capacity for self-replication. Memes represent an attempt to apply evolutionary theory to culture, but cultural evolution, if there is such a thing, is blind. The cultural transmission of memes is as directionless a process as the natural selection of genes.

Theories of cultural evolution may be tosh, but they have had an enduring appeal. The reason is not hard to find: they identify evolution with progress. They are formulated in the language of science, but the need they answer is not a need for truth. It is to find meaning and purpose in history. The Christian myth of salvation in history did not vanish with the arrival of secular thought. On the contrary, it has shaped secular thinking, giving rise to the idea of progress that inspired many of the political movements of the past century.

Now that faith in politics is dead, secular cultures have pinned their hopes on science. The reality of scientific progress cannot be seriously disputed – it is demonstrated by the fact of increasing human power – but that does not mean that it can be replicated in society at large. Science cannot end the conflicts of history. It is an instrument that humans use to achieve their goals, whether winning wars or curing the sick, alleviating poverty or committing genocide. To think that it can ever be otherwise is to envisage a transformation in human affairs as miraculous as any expected by the millenarian movements of the late Middle Ages. The belief that science can bring about a new world is a secular myth, and further from the enduring realities of human life than almost any of the myths of the past.

The biblical story of the Fall is closer to the truth. Knowledge is not an unmixed good; it can be as much a curse as a blessing. If the superseded science of the first half of the twentieth century could be used to wage two hideously destructive world wars, how will the vastly superior science of today be used? After all, there is no sign of the human animal changing its ways. We would surely be better off without the powers of destruction that science has already given us, let alone those we will acquire as scientific advance accelerates. I doubt we can return to the myths of the past and I am not sure we should try. But which is the greater leap of faith: to accept that humanity has eaten from the tree of knowledge and must somehow live with the consequences, or to believe that science can deliver humanity from itself?

December 15, 2003

8

A REPORT TO THE ACADEMY

In Kafka's story 'A Report to an Academy', an ape called Red Peter delivers a lecture to a learned society in which he gives an account of the life he led before he acquired human ways. Captured on the Gold Coast (now Ghana), Red Peter was transported in a cage to Hamburg. In that city, he reports, he faced two alternatives: the zoological gardens or the variety stage. Life in the zoological gardens meant only another cage, so he chose the stage. It was not easy to get into the variety hall, but once there Red Peter was an enormous success. Soon he learnt to talk like a human, and it was not long before he achieved what he termed 'the cultural level of an average European'. His stage performances enabled him to enjoy a distinctly human way of life. As he described it in his report to the academy: 'When I come home late at night from banquets, from scientific receptions, from social gatherings, there sits waiting for me a half-trained little chimpanzee, and I take comfort from her as apes do.'

Kafka's story is cited in J M Coetzee's *The Lives of Animals*, a profound fictional meditation on the contradictions that beset our attitudes to other animal species. The story of Red Peter is a fantastical version of the fate that befell many apes, and, as one of Coetzee's characters notes, there were real-life prototypes of Red Peter. In 1912, the Prussian Academy established a research centre on the island of Tenerife to study the mental powers of apes; and in 1917, the director of the centre, Wolfgang Kohler, published some of the results of this in his celebrated study *The Mentality of Apes*. Like Red Peter, Kohler's apes underwent a period of training designed to induce them to adopt human ways. Among the pedagogic methods used was slow starvation, with the apes being repeatedly shown and denied food until they developed something resembling human faculties.

It is not clear how researchers today would assess the results of this experiment, but Kohler, one of the founders of cognitive psychology, seems to have seen it as a success, noting with satisfaction how the captive chimpanzees ran in a circle round their compound, some draped in old strips of cloth and others carrying pieces of rubbish, 'for all the world like a military band'.

Kohler's experiments were cruel and demeaning to the animals on which they were inflicted, but they are chiefly notable for the deep confusion they exhibit in his, and our, view of our closest evolutionary kin. We have come to view apes as protohumans, yet we subject them to treatment we would not dream of inflicting on members of our own species. If apes were not similar to us in important respects, many of the experiments to which they are subjected would be impossible or pointless. Few now deny that apes share much of our intellectual and emotional inheritance. They have many of our own capacities and vulnerabilities: they can think and plan, and they feel fear and love. Without these similarities, Kohler's experiments would not have been possible. Yet these very similarities undercut the ethical basis of such experimentation.

We do not put humans into captivity and starve them in order to test their intellectual abilities because we know that such treatment would cause severe suffering. How can we justify such experimentation on apes, knowing that it can work only to the extent that their capacities, including the capacity to suffer, are much like our own? Can there be any compelling ethical defence of using creatures so like ourselves in ways that we would find unbearable? Or is the answer that the animals used in such experiments are simply unfortunate, that we have them in our power and their suffering is a regrettable but unavoidable result of our using them for our benefit?

The last of these options appears to have been taken recently by a spokesman for Cambridge University. Responding to protests against plans to establish a primate research centre there, he observed that it is an unfortunate fact that only primates have brains like our own. The implication is that it is precisely because apes have many of the capacities of humans that they are used for experimentation. It is true that experimenting on primates is a productive research technique; but if their similarities with us justify using apes in this way, it would surely be even more effective to use humans. The argument for experimenting on primates leads inexorably to the conclusion that it is permissible – in fact, preferable – to experimenting on humans.

Quite rightly, the idea that humans should be used in painful or dangerous medical experiments evokes intense moral horror; but this has not always been so. Powerless and marginal people in prisons and mental hospitals, for example, have in the past often been used as guinea pigs, and it is all too easy to imagine the forcible use of humans in scientific research practised on a far wider scale. The Nazis saw nothing wrong in subjecting members of what they considered to be inferior populations to the most horrible experiments; and there can be little doubt that had the outcome of the Second World War been different, the use of humans for scientific research would have been institutionalized across Europe. No doubt it would have been condemned by a dedicated few, but the historical experience of occupied Europe suggests that the majority of the population would have accepted the practice.

It will be objected that there is a vital difference between using animals for scientific research and using humans: humans have the capacity for consent, whereas animals do not. It is true that adult humans can express their wishes to other humans in ways that even our closest animal kin cannot; but consent is not the heart of the matter. Even if they agreed, it would be morally intolerable to use prison inmates in dangerous medical experiments. No form of consent they might give could make the injury done to them less real; it would only reflect their powerlessness. Similarly, it is not the inability of human infants to give their consent that justifies an absolute ban on experimenting on them. It is the terrible damage we would inflict on them merely to produce benefits for ourselves.

The same is true of experiments on animals. It is not the capacity for consent that is most relevant, but the capacity for suffering. I am no Utilitarian, but Jeremy Bentham hit the spot when he wrote of animals that the crucial question is not 'Can they speak?'. Rather, it is 'Can they suffer?'.

At this point, those who support animal experimentation have a habit of wheeling out some extremely familiar arguments. Animals lack the capacity for personal autonomy, they tell us, and so cannot recognize duties to others. For the same reason, they cannot have rights. Humans have the power of choice, and this entitles them to a moral status denied to other animal species.

We hear this tired refrain whenever the subject of animals is discussed, but it is significant not so much for any intellectual content it may have, but for what it shows about the lingering influence of religious belief. If you are a Christian, it makes perfect sense to think of humans as standing in a different category from other animals. Humans have free will and an immortal soul, and these attributes confer an incomparable importance on human life. No doubt we should refrain from gratuitous cruelty to other creatures, but they have no claim to value in their own right; they are instruments for achieving human ends. Humans have dominion over animals because humans alone are made in the image of God.

Secular thinkers find it extremely difficult to come up with reasons for thinking that the human species has some kind of unique standing in the world. Darwin showed that we share a common lineage with other animals, and subsequent genetic research has shown the closeness of these evolutionary links. Insofar as humans do have morally relevant attributes that other animals lack, it is right to treat them differently. But within a purely secular perspective there can be no good reason for thinking the human species is supremely valuable.

In the context of their beliefs about animals, as in many other areas, secular humanists parrot a Christian hymn of human uniqueness. They prattle on about the supreme value of human personality as if it were a self-evident truth. Yet it is not accepted in most of the world's religions, and is strikingly absent in some, such as Buddhism, that have never thought of other species as mere instruments of human purposes. Secular humanists are adopting the anthropocentric viewpoint of Christianity, while abandoning the theistic belief system from which it sprang, and without which it is meaningless.

Once Christianity and humanism have been set aside, it becomes clear that the chief difference between humans and other animals is simply that humans have acquired enormous power. In evolutionary terms, the human species has been an astonishing success. In the space of a few thousand years, it has achieved a seeming mastery over its environment, which is reflected in a vast increase in human population. At the same time, humans have had a huge, and almost entirely harmful, impact on other animal species. The mass extinction of wildlife we are seeing throughout the world comes from the destruction of habitat, itself largely a result of rising human numbers. The damage done to the welfare of other animal species by human expansion is on an incomparably larger scale than anything that is done in scientific laboratories. This does not mean vivisection is unimportant or that it should not be prohibited. After all, no one thinks that since millions of people are slaughtered in wars it does not matter if some die as a result of murder. It does mean that anyone who focuses narrowly on animal experimentation is missing the big picture.

The chief threat to animal welfare today comes from the unchecked expansion of *homo rapiens*. Wherever humans have entered a new environment the result has been a wave of extinctions. This is what happened when Polynesian settlers arrived in New Zealand a few hundred years ago, and it was the arrival of humans in North America around 12,000 years ago that accounts for the disappearance of about 70 per cent of its large mammals. Though some hunter-gatherer cultures may have reached a precarious balance with the natural world and a number of Buddhist peoples have displayed remarkable self-restraint in their treatment of animals, the history of human relations with other species is a record of almost unbroken rapacity. Wrecking the environment seems to be in the nature of the beast.

This may seem a despairing conclusion, but for anyone whose horizons are not confined to the human world, there are grounds for hope. While humans have enormous power over the environment, their capacity to control it is strictly limited. The present level of human population depends on maintaining high levels of industrial production, but global warming will prevent world-wide industrialization on anything resembling the dominant western model. There is no way that eight billion people can have the lifestyle that has come into being in a few countries over the past century or so.

Most green thinkers believe that this transition can come about as a result of political action, and there are some policies that would help. By far the most effective way of limiting human numbers is giving women control of their own fertility. Making contraception and abortion universally available enhances human well-being and at the same time reduces the pressures that are destroying animal habitat. Population control should be central in any programme of transition to a more stable world and, in fact, many developing countries have population policies. However, the subject is surrounded with an aura of political incorrectness. As a result, it has become fashionable to talk as if a sustainable way of life can be achieved simply by shifting to a different economic system. In reality, finite resources impose insuperable limits on the growth of human numbers and the Earth's carrying capacity has probably already been breached.

One way or another, human expansion will be curbed; and a plausible scenario is that this will occur as a by-product of war. Globalization supports the present high levels of human population, but its logic is to intensify the struggle for scarce natural resources. Resource wars, such as the two Gulf wars, look set to dominate the coming century. Such conflicts would be damaging to animals as well as humans, but because of their disruptive effect on the global supply chain, their impact on humans could well be much more severe. The end result could be a less crowded world in which other species have room to breathe. *Homo rapiens* is a ferociously destructive creature, but its capacity for self-destruction is even greater. The human behaviour that Wolfgang Kohler was so pleased to observe being parodied by his captive apes may yet prove to be the ultimate guarantee of animal liberation.

February 9, 2004

PART 2

WAR, TERRORISM AND IRAQ

9

9/11: HISTORY RESUMES

The dozen years between the fall of the Wall and the assault on the Twin Towers will be remembered as an era of delusion. The west greeted the collapse of communism – though it was itself a western ideology – as the triumph of western values. The end of the most catastrophic utopian experiment in history was welcomed as a historic opportunity to launch yet another vast utopian project, a global free market. Now, after the attacks on New York and Washington, we are back on the classical terrain of history, where war is waged not over ideologies, but over religion, ethnicity, territory and the control of natural resources.

We are in for a long period – not months but years, perhaps decades – of acutely dangerous conflict, from which it will be impossible, as well as wrong, for Britain to stand aside. It will be a type of conflict with which many regions of the world are all too familiar, but which overturns many of our preconceptions about war and peace. Its protagonists are not the agents of states, but organizations whose relationships with governments are oblique, ambiguous and sometimes indecipherable. The men who struck the Pentagon and the World Trade

Center, using penknives and passenger jets as weapons, were soldiers in a new kind of war.

A monopoly of organized violence is one of the defining powers of the modern state, achieved slowly and with difficulty. Now war, like so much else in the age of globalization, has slipped from the control of governments, and it has done so, moreover, with astonishing speed. The world is littered with collapsed states; in much of Africa, in Afghanistan, in the Balkans and a good deal of Russia, there is nothing that resembles a modern state. In these zones of anarchy, wars are fought by irregular armies commanded by political and religious organizations, often clan-based, and prone to savage internecine conflicts. No power is strong enough to enforce peace.

The results expose the weaknesses and contradictions of the global free market constructed after the cold war. Rich societies cannot be insulated from the collapsed states and the new forms of war they breed. Asylum-seekers and economic refugees press on the borders of every advanced country. But while trade and capital move freely across the globe, the movement of labour is strictly limited – a very different state of affairs from the late nineteenth century, a period of comparable globalization in which barriers to immigration hardly existed. This is a contradiction rarely noted by tub-thumpers for the global market, but it will become more acute as travel is monitored and controlled ever more stringently by governments.

With the assaults on New York and Washington, the anarchy that has been one of the by-products of globalization in much of the world can no longer be ignored. The ragged armies of the world's most collapsed zones have proved that they can reach to the heart of its most powerful state. Their brutal coup is an example of what military analysts call 'asymmetric threat' – in other words, the power of the weak against the strong. What it has shown is that the strong are weaker than anyone imagined.

The powerlessness of the strong is not new. It has long been revealed in the futile 'war' on drugs. The traffic in illegal drugs is, along with oil and armaments, one of the three largest components of world trade. Like other branches of organized crime, it has thrived in the free-for-all created by financial deregulation. The world's richest states have squandered billions on a vain crusade against a highly globalized and fabulously well-funded industry. Rooting out terrorism will be even more difficult. After all, most of the worst effects of the drug trade can be eradicated simply by legalizing it. There is no parallel remedy for terrorism.

The atrocities in Washington and New York did more than reveal the laxity of America's airport security and the limitations of its intelligence agencies. It inflicted a grievous blow to the beliefs that underpin the global market. In the past, it was taken for granted that the world will always be a dangerous place. Investors knew that war and revolution could wipe out their profits at any time. Over the past decade, under the influence of absurd theories about new paradigms and the end of history, they came to believe that the worldwide advance of commercial liberalism was irresistible; financial markets priced assets accordingly. The effect of the attack on the World Trade Center may be about to do what none of the crises of the past few years – the Asian crisis, the Russian default of 1998 and the collapse of Long Term Capital Management, an overleveraged hedge fund – was able to do. It may shatter the markets' own faith in globalization.

Some people say that this was the purpose of the attack, and that we would be craven to give in to it. Instead, we are told, we must reassert the verities of the global free market and seek to rebuild it. And, with luck, it may not be too late to stave off worldwide recession. But the name of the game has changed: the entire view of the world that supported the markets' faith in globalization has melted down. Whatever anyone tells you, it cannot be reconstituted. The wiser course is to ask what was wrong with it.

It is worth reminding ourselves how grandiose were the dreams of the globalizers. The entire world was to be remade as a universal free market. No matter how different their histories and values, however deep their differences or bitter their conflicts, all cultures everywhere were to be corralled into a universal civilization.

What is striking is how closely the market liberal philosophy that underpins globalization resembles Marxism. Both are essentially secular religions, in which the eschatological hopes and fantasies of Christianity are given an Enlightenment twist. In both, history is understood as the progress of the species, powered by growing knowledge and wealth, and culminating in a universal civilization. Human beings are viewed primarily in economic terms, as producers or consumers, with – at bottom – the same values and needs. Religion of the old-fashioned sort is seen as peripheral, destined soon to disappear, or to shrink into the private sphere, where it can no longer affect politics or inflame war.

History's crimes and tragedies are not thought to have their roots in human nature: they are errors, mistakes that can be corrected by more education, better political institutions, higher living standards. Marxists and market liberals may differ as to what is the best economic system, but for both, vested interests and human irrationality alone stand between humankind and a radiant future. In holding to this primitive Enlightenment creed, they are at one.

And both have their dogmatic, missionary side. For market liberals, there is only one way to become modern. All societies must adopt free markets. If their religious beliefs or their patterns of family life make this difficult for them, too bad – that is their problem. If the individualist values that free markets require and propagate go with high levels of inequality and crime, and if some sections of society go to the wall, tough – that is the price of progress. If entire countries are ruined, as happened in Russia during the time of neo-liberal shock therapy, well – as an earlier generation of utopian thinkers nonchalantly put it – you can't make an omelette without breaking eggs.

During the 1990s, this crudely rationalistic philosophy was hugely influential. It had a stronghold in the International Monetary Fund, as it blundered and bungled its way across the world imposing identical policies on countries with utterly different histories, problems and circumstances. There was only one route to modernity, and the seers who ruled the IMF were resolved that it be followed everywhere.

In fact, there are many ways of being modern, and many of failing to be so. It is simply not true that liberal capitalism is the only way of organizing a modern economy. Bismarck's Prussia embodied a different model, as did tsarist Russia, and each of them might well have been with us still in some form had the First World War ended differently. The Japanese and German forms of capitalism have never conformed to the free market model and, despite orthodox opinion everywhere telling us the contrary, it is a safe bet that they never will. We cannot know in advance what modernity means for any given society, or what it takes to achieve it. All we know for sure is that different countries have modernised successfully in a variety of ways.

The atrocities of 11 September have planted a question mark over the very idea of modernity. Is it really the case that all societies are bound, sooner or later, to converge on the same values and views of the world? Not only in America but also, to some degree, in most western countries, the belief that modernization is a historical imperative that no society can ignore for long made it harder to perceive the growing risk of an anti-western backlash. Led by the US, the world's richest states have acted on the assumption that people everywhere want to live as they do. As a result, they failed to recognize the deadly mixture of emotions – cultural resentment, the sense of injustice and a genuine rejection of western modernity – that lies behind the attacks on New York and Washington.

In my view, it is reasonable to regard the struggle against the groups that mounted those attacks as a defence of civilized values. As their destruction of ancient Buddhist relics demonstrated, the Taliban are hostile to the very ideas of toleration and pluralism. But these ideas are not the property of any one civilization – and they are not even peculiarly modern. In western countries, the practice of toleration owes much to the Reformation and, indeed, to the Enlightenment, which has always contained a sceptical tradition alongside its more dogmatic schools. Beyond Europe, toleration flourished long before the modern era in the Muslim kingdoms of Moorish

Spain and Buddhist India, to name only two examples. It would be a fatal error to interpret the conflict that is now under way in terms of poisonous theories about clashing civilizations.

Effective action against terrorism must have the support of a broad coalition of states, of which Britain should certainly be part. Crucially, these must include Muslim countries (which is one reason why American military action must entail new attempts to seek peace in Israel). Constructing such a far-reaching alliance will be an exercise in realpolitik in which ideas of global governance of the kind that have lately been fashionable on the left become largely irrelevant. The US will find itself supping with former enemies and courting states that are in no sense committed to liberal values. In waging war against the Taliban, it will do battle against a force it backed only a few years ago to resist the Soviet invasion. Such ironies can no more be conjured away by international courts than by global markets. They are built into an intractably disordered world. Bodies such as the United Nations can play a useful role in the labyrinthine diplomacy that will inevitably surround military action. But anyone who thinks that this crisis is an opportunity to rebuild world order on a liberal model has not understood it. The ideal of a universal civilization is a recipe for unending conflict, and it is time it was given up. What is urgently needed is an attempt to work out terms of civilized coexistence among cultures and regimes that will always be different.

Over the coming years, the transnational institutions that have built the global free market will have to accept a more modest role, or else they will find themselves among the casualties of this great upheaval. The notion that trade and wealth creation require global laissez-faire has no basis in history. The cold war – a time of controls on capital and extensive intervention in the economy by national governments – was, in western countries, a time of unprecedented prosperity. Contrary to the cranky orthodoxies of market liberals, capitalism does not need a worldwide free market to thrive. It needs a reasonably secure environment, safe from the threat of major war, and reliable rules about the conduct of business. These things cannot be provided by the brittle structures of the global free market.

On the contrary, the attempt to force life everywhere into a single mould is bound to fuel conflict and insecurity. As far as possible, rules on trade and the movement of capital should be left to agreements between sovereign states. If countries opt to stay out of global markets, they should be left in peace. They should be free to find their own version of modernity, or not to modernise at all. So long as they pose no threat to others, even intolerable regimes should be tolerated. A looser, more fragmented world would be a less tidy world. It would also be a safer world.

It will be objected that this defies the dominant trend of the age. But while it is true that technology will continue to shrink time and distance, and in that sense link the world more closely, it is only a bankrupt philosophy of history that leads people to think that it will produce convergence on values, let alone a world-wide civilization.

Globalization makes the world smaller, it does not make it more peaceful. On the contrary, new weapons of mass destruction can – and quite possibly will – be used to prosecute old-style wars of religion. The Enlightenment thinking that found expression in the era of globalization will not be much use in its dangerous aftermath. Even Hobbes cannot tell us how to deal with fundamentalist warriors who choose certain death in order to humble their enemies. The lesson of 11 September is that the go-go years of globalization were an interregnum, a time of transition between two epochs of conflict. The task in front of us is to forge terms of peace among peoples separated by divergent histories, beliefs and values. In the perilous years to come, this more-than-Hobbesian labour will be quite enough to keep us occupied.

September 24, 2002

10

THE DECADENCE OF MARKET POWER

In Buenos Aires, I met the last finance minister to serve the government of the dictator Juan Peron. I asked him what had been the most important change in his country during the past 50 years. 'The decline of the army as a political force,' he replied. And the next major development? The elegant old man smiled. 'The decadence of market power.'

Since that conversation, market power has gone into retreat in many parts of the world. As the old man foresaw, International Monetary Fund policies, which aimed for stability in Argentina's public finances, destabilized the country politically, triggered a middle-class revolt and created near-anarchy. The Argentinian meltdown has sent tremors throughout Latin America, with even populist rulers such as Hugo Chavez of Venezuela suddenly insecure as power shifts to the streets. In Japan, a 1930s-style debt deflation is likely to result in the nationalization, in effect, of the banking system.

In the United States itself, the Bush administration has unceremoniously shredded the Washington consensus on the virtues of global free trade by imposing tariffs on imported steel; Alan Greenspan, the chairman of the Federal Reserve, has gone for a hyper-Keynesian policy of reflation at any cost;

and defence spending, as well as tax cuts, are consuming the federal surplus. Monetary and fiscal rectitude may be all very well for countries such as Argentina; it counts for nothing when the world's largest economy is at risk. Governments may still bow to the icons of the free market, but their actions tell a different story. Throughout the world, market forces are being subordinated to the imperatives of war and politics.

This will not surprise anyone with a smattering of history. The fantasy that the world could become one big free market can be indulged only in a time of boom. I am confident that, a few years from now, there will be not a single person who admits to having ever entertained such a ridiculous delusion. Yet with political thinking stuck between the swivel-eyed enthusiasms of the free-market right and the befogged respectability of the centre left, we have hardly begun to consider what the decay of market power will mean for the world.

We can make a start by clearing our minds of fashionable cant. We need to distinguish sharply and clearly between the pressure for a worldwide free market and the process of globalization. Contrary to conventional wisdom, the two do not move in the same direction, but rather the reverse. The global free market is a political project that is not much more than a decade old; globalization dates back at least to the late nineteenth century, when transatlantic telegraph cables provided, for the first time, an instant link between markets in Europe and North America.

Properly understood, globalization means nothing more than the increasing interconnection of world events, created by technologies that abolish or curtail time and distance. Because it is driven by new technologies, it is an inexorable process. One of its by-products is the spread of the weapons of mass destruction that so urgently, and to my mind rightly, concerns the Bush administration. Determined to concentrate on the threats to US national security that flow from the diffusion of destructive technologies, Washington is losing interest in projecting its model of capitalism on to other countries. In this, as in other contexts, the impact of globalization is to undermine the worldwide free market.

Last year's attacks on Washington and New York were carried out with simple tools that are widely available; but the world that 11 September revealed is one in which technologies of enormous destructive potential are slipping from the control of states. One must presume that al-Qaeda lacks nuclear and biological warfare capability, because if it had such weapons, it would have used them by now. But there can be no doubt that al-Qaeda and the successor networks that are surely springing up in its wake will do all they can to acquire such a capability. Stopping them will be an extremely formidable task: the knowledge needed to make these weapons is dispersed in hundreds of universities and thousands of commercial enterprises, and the technical processes involved are becoming cheaper by the day.

But the difficulties of controlling the spread of destructive technologies are magnified in the chaotic environment created by weakened governments and uncontrolled capital flows. In a semi-anarchic global market, it is almost impossible to track terrorist funds, or prevent organized crime becoming a channel for the transmission of potentially dangerous materials. Although our politicians have yet to admit it, the war on terrorism cannot be prosecuted effectively so long as the global market remains as unregulated as it is today.

*

If the US is quietly shelving the programme of worldwide trade and financial deregulation that so energized it over the past decade, the IMF and the World Bank have yet to notice. They continue to chant the market mantras of the 1980s and 1990s.

The reason is not just institutional inertia. The global free market still has a powerful ideological appeal. Policies in transnational institutions are still shaped by the belief that there is an ideal type of market economy towards which all actually existing economies are slowly evolving. Like the communists of former times, who spent their lives in the delusion that they were the vanguard of a new era in history, the bureaucratic missionaries of the IMF and the World Bank see themselves as the midwives of a new global economy. But whereas it is certain that economic activity throughout the world will become ever more closely interlinked, it is no less certain that the world will never converge on a single economic system.

The world's diverse economies are outgrowths of different patterns of family life, religious beliefs and political histories. Economic systems compete with one another, but it is rare for economic factors to decide their success or failure; war and resultant shifts of regime are usually more important. Economic failings did not end Soviet central planning; the military challenge of Ronald Reagan's Star Wars, together with the political challenge of nationalism in Poland and the Baltic states, was far more important. In much the same way, we can be sure that the brittle structures of the global free market will not survive the crises and dislocations of a new era of war.

The world is not evolving into a single type of market economy. Market individualism remains only one kind of economic culture, and it is not one that globalization necessarily favours. On the contrary, it is often groups animated by what are conventionally seen as pre-modern values that do best. In recent years, the informal banking systems of many Asian and Islamic countries have expanded throughout the world. Relying on trust rather than contracts, and held together by religious and clan loyalties, these community-based credit unions have enabled immigrants to survive and prosper in many countries. They have also sometimes served as conduits for funds that end up in the hands of groups such as al-Qaeda. Globalization has no tendency to strengthen individualist values. Partly for that reason, there has never been any reason to believe that it will lead to the universal reach of the free market.

Defenders of neo-liberal orthodoxy bang on apocalyptically about the disastrous consequences if the global economic regime breaks down. What is actually happening is a reversion to historical normalcy.

The international landscape at the start of the twenty-first century has a good deal in common with that in the last decades of the nineteenth century. As in the nineteenth century, international conflicts are rooted in religious and ethnic enmities and in competition for natural resources, rather than in political ideologies. Now, as then, the great powers act partly in concert and partly as strategic rivals. Where British international hegemony in the late nineteenth century was based on naval power, America's global dominance today rests on its unchallengeable superiority in high-tech military action.

But this does not, as is often argued, make the US uniquely and unassailably strong. Unlike nineteenth-century Britain, which exported capital throughout the world, the US – the world's largest debtor – is crucially dependent on inflows of capital from other countries. Moreover, though one can scarcely exaggerate its lead in military hardware, this is unlikely to be decisive in the asymmetric warfare which at present chiefly threatens it. A new version of Reagan's scheme for a space-based missile defence system could not have prevented 11 September, nor will it stop far worse attacks involving small, home-made nuclear devices. Moreover, even America's unchallengeable lead in the most expensive military assets will be eroded over time. Pax Americana may prove to be no more durable than Pax Britannica – perhaps less so.

Unlike some in Europe, I do not welcome a weakening of US power. A multi-polar world may be fine in theory: in present circumstances, it is a recipe for international anarchy. An American imperium is the only form of global governance on offer, and it is surely more benign than any alternative one can realistically imagine.

But if there is not to be a rerun of conflicts of the kind that led to the First World War, the US will need to exercise extraordinary restraint. It will have to renounce the attempt to make over the world in its own image and accept that there will always be a diversity of regimes and economic systems, some of which will be alien or hostile to American values. If its vast military assets are to be deployed, that should be in defence of clear and definite national interests, not as part of a messianic crusade to save the world.

This is one respect in which the Bush administration cannot be faulted. Whatever one may think of some of the rhetoric that has accompanied it, the actual conduct of the war on terrorism so far has been prudent and restrained. Better the Hobbesian clarity of Donald Rumsfeld than the unpredictability and bombast of Bill Clinton.

The real worry concerns the next phase of the war. An attack on Iraq may be justified in order to prevent Saddam Hussein building up his armoury of weapons of mass destruction, but it is fraught with fearful risks. Unlike Afghanistan, Iraq is a well-entrenched modern police state. Unlike the Taliban, Saddam Hussein may already possess certain weapons of mass destruction which he will not hesitate to use in a conflict he cannot hope to survive. (How many US body bags is George Bush's government willing to accept as the price of completing unfinished business in Iraq?)

The impact on the Middle East of an American-led attack on Iraq is incalculable. Will governments that support it, or seem to acquiesce to it, be able to suppress popular dissent? Or will a pre-emptive American assault on Iraq trigger regime changes in other countries? One significant reason why George Bush Snr did not press on to Baghdad was a fear that toppling Saddam might lead to the fragmentation of the Iraqi state. Is that fear less well founded today? An assault on Iraq could well end any hope, however faint, for a peaceful resolution of the Palestinian question. In fact, the clear danger is that it could spark a conflagration in the Middle East.

The larger issue that is posed by these questions concerns the conditions of peace in a time when globalization and state failure have gone hand in hand. I have compared current circumstances to those of the late nineteenth century, but what is without precedent is the global reach of organized violence that is beyond any state control. A good deal of terrorist activity remains national or regional in focus, but networks such as al-Qaeda are distinctive and novel in that they can project themselves world-wide, and thrive in places where the state is corroded or collapsed.

Unconventional warfare of this new globalized variety cannot be dealt with by forcing changes of regime in countries where the state has failed. The result is merely to replace one powerless government by another. This much is clear in Afghanistan. Neither the allied military forces nor the new Afghan government has much leverage over the day-to-day conduct of the war on the ground, which is determined largely by shifting alliances among the country's warlords. There cannot be peace in Afghanistan without an effective state; but creating a modern state in countries where it has been destroyed, or never existed, cannot be done in a day.

The decay of market power that is now under way creates a new set of conditions for which mainstream opinion is ill prepared. Politicians on both left and right have succumbed to the illusion that globalization is leading the world into an era of peace and plenty, in which the state will play a diminished part.

The reality is almost the opposite. Unchecked globalization results in a semi-anarchic environment that threatens even the strongest states. In a predictable counter-movement, we are entering a new era of state power.

March 25, 2002

11

JOSEPH CONRAD, OUR CONTEMPORARY

'The sacrosanct fetish of today is science.' Mr Vladimir, first secretary at the Russian embassy in Joseph Conrad's novel *The Secret Agent*, believes that if terrorism is to be truly effective, it must be directed against the spirit of the age. In order to have any real impact, a bomb outrage must be purely destructive – an attack on society's most deeply cherished beliefs. Believing it to be 'in some mysterious way at the source of their material prosperity', both bourgeois public opinion and society's most radical critics regard science with deep reverence. Accordingly, Mr Vladimir instructs his *agent provocateur*, Adolf Verloc, to blow up the Royal Observatory at Greenwich: 'Go for the first meridian. You don't know the middle classes as well as I do. Their sensibilities are jaded. The first meridian. Nothing better, and nothing easier, I should think.' Attacking a building dedicated to the science of astronomy would be 'an act of destructive ferocity so absurd as to be incomprehensible, inexplicable, almost unthinkable', but it would be effective for that very reason: 'Madness alone is truly terrifying, inasmuch as you cannot placate it either by threats, persuasion or bribes.'

In *The Secret Agent*, Conrad makes use of an actual terrorist attempt on the Royal Observatory in 1894, when a French anarchist accidentally blew himself up in Greenwich Park before reaching his target. At the start of the twenty-first century, science remains a sacrosanct fetish. We believe the Internet is the source of our prosperity, linking up economic life everywhere in a network of beneficial exchange. At the same time, in a development that attests to the power of Conrad's darkly ironic vision, the symbols of trade and new technology have come under terrorist attack. On 11 September 2001, the suicide-warriors of al-Qaeda carried off a terrifying assault on the spirit of the age of precisely the kind that Mr Vladimir recommended.

Conrad published *The Secret Agent* in 1907. He took his subject matter from the anxieties of his time: the ambiguities of progress and civilization; the sense of the blind drift of history that preceded the First World War; and the break-up of personal identity that comes with loss of faith in the future. For much of the past hundred years, these seemed dated themes, with little bearing on the great political transformations that preoccupied novelists such as George Orwell and Arthur Koestler. Whatever horrors they chronicled, Orwell and Koestler never gave up the hope that humankind could have a better future. It did not occur to them that history might be cyclical, not progressive, with the struggles of earlier eras returning and being played out against a background of increased scientific knowledge and technological power. For all their dystopian forebodings, neither anticipated the twenty-first-century reality, in which ethnic and religious wars have supplanted secular ideological conflicts, terror has returned to the most advanced societies and empire is being reinvented.

Conrad, by contrast, scorned the nineteenth and twentieth-century faith in revolutionary political change. Yet precisely

because he never accepted that collective action could fundamentally transform the conditions of human life, he
anticipated more clearly than any twentieth-century writer the
dilemmas that face us today. He can be read as the first great
political novelist of the twenty-first century.

Conrad spurned the idea of progress. Writing to Bertrand
Russell, who had pinned his hopes for the future on international socialism, he declared that it was 'the sort of thing to
which I cannot attach any definite meaning. I have never been
able to find in any man's book or any man's talk anything con-
vincing enough to stand up for a moment against my
deep-seated sense of fatality governing this man-inhabited
world.' This sense of the fated character of human life was
reflected in Conrad's portrayal of revolutionaries, whom he
viewed as shams who renew the crimes and delusions of the
society they seek to destroy.

Verloc, in *The Secret Agent*, thinks of himself as a respectable
family man. A dealer in pornography, a police informer and a
spy working for a foreign embassy, he believes his work con-
tributes to social and political stability. In this, he is no different
from his controller, Vladimir, who directs him to commit bomb
outrages so as to force the English (whom he views as over-
tolerant to the point of decadence) to defend the social order
by repression. Yet Verloc is murdered by his wife, Winnie, after
she discovers he has caused the death of her brother, the mentally retarded and hypersensitive Stevie, by using him to place
the bomb at Greenwich.

Conrad's scorn for revolutionaries is comprehensive and
unremitting. He represents Verloc as a man whose life is ruled
by indolence and a perversely refined notion of respectability.
Much the same is true of Verloc's revolutionary comrade

Ossipon, who is described as a weakling who lives by exploiting the vulnerability of women. All of these professed revolutionaries are shown as being hopelessly compromised by the same vices that permeate the society they reject.

Even the book's most sympathetically portrayed anarchist, the Professor, is presented in terms that are half-comic. His beliefs are a ragbag of the pseudo-scientific superstitions of the time, such as Lombroso's theories of inherited criminal degeneracy and the bastardization of Darwinian ideas to supply a rationale for exterminating the weak. Like many progressive thinkers, the Professor affects a lucidity of thought that is devoid of sentimentality. In fact, his thinking is credulous and self-indulgent, shaped by a naïve positivist belief in science not much different from the faith in progress that animated the Victorian social order he despised. His fate goes unrecorded, but it seems likely that, like the weaker Comrade Ossipon, he will end 'marching in the gutter as if in training for the task of an inevitable future', shoulders bowed, 'ready to receive the leather yoke of the sandwich board'.

Unlike Dostoevsky, by whom he was much influenced, but whose Christianity he found repugnant, Conrad saw no redemption for revolutionists. To him, revolutionary violence was vain, deluded and inherently criminal. But nor did he believe in the fundamental health of the society that revolutionaries tried to disturb. In Conrad's radically Hobbesian view, social institutions are themselves tainted with criminality. Society is a dim battleground of predatory and fragmentary egos, in which self-interest and self-deception leave nothing untouched. Thus, in *The Secret Agent*, Conrad portrays London as a sightless wasteland, where 'the dust of humanity settles inert and hopeless out of the stream of life', and human hopes are consumed in the everyday struggle for survival. But his most direct statement of the inherently criminal aspect of every social enterprise is in *Heart of Darkness*, his celebrated fable of imperialism.

A great deal of ink has been spilt attacking Conrad's views on colonialism, but it is safe to say that few, if any, of Conrad's twentieth-century critics had the imagination to anticipate that the age of empire could return. With an irony Conrad would have appreciated, however, that is what is happening today. Partly as a matter of self-defence and partly for familiar reasons that have to do with the control of natural resources, the world's great powers are reviving the imperial projects of the nineteenth century. There are differences between then and now, some of them vast. Today's great powers include countries that were subject to western rule in Conrad's day, notably China and India, and, though it is at present economically weak, Japan remains potentially hugely powerful. These parts of the world will not return to European or western hegemony. The new imperialism centres on regions where states have collapsed, with damaging spill-over effects on migration, crime and terrorism.

Equally significantly, the Great Game seems to have become less dangerously competitive. With the shared goals of countering terrorism and securing control of central Asia's reserves of oil and natural gas, Russia and the US appear to have entered a long-term strategic partnership. Furthermore, the great powers are now to some degree inhibited by the danger of exposure in the mass media, and by the need to legitimize intervention through transnational organizations. These differences have led some to argue that the new imperialism will not revive the exploitative rule of a century ago: rather, it will supply desperately needed benefits, otherwise beyond reach, to people living in failed states. This is the view expressed by Robert Cooper, an adviser to the Prime Minister, in a recent pamphlet for the Blairite Foreign Policy Centre.

The merit of his line of thought is that it candidly faces the realities of state failure that have for too long been evaded. But it is impossible to suppress a sense of irony about the prospects of the new imperialism: not the fashionable kind of irony that takes nothing seriously, but the irony explored in Conrad's writings – the unintended consequences and inevitable moral ambiguity of all our enterprises. This is a pervasive feature of his interpretation of imperialism. As Conrad pictures him, Kurtz – the ivory trader at the Inner Station in *Heart of Darkness* – is corrupt, power-obsessed and hardly sane. Yet Conrad also describes him as 'essentially a great musician', and wrote: 'All Europe contributed to the making of Kurtz.'

Conrad had no illusions about the civilizing mission that was invoked to justify imperialism in the nineteenth century. He knew that European expansion into Africa was fuelled by much baser motives. Yet Conrad also shows how it emerged from, and worked to undermine, the European sense of self. The dissolution of civilized values that occurred in the Belgian Congo was a disaster for its inhabitants. At the same time, it exposed the illusions – of progress, enlightenment and universal humanity – that shape the modern European self-image.

What is truly distinctive about Conrad's perspective is that he does not view this development as somehow liberating. Taking their cue from Christianity, European progressives imagine that perceiving the darker side of civilization enables us to move on to higher levels of enlightenment. Conrad accepts no such redemption. Always finding Christianity distasteful (he once described it as an 'absurd oriental fable'), he rejects the idea that we can improve our condition by understanding it better. For him, this humanist faith is only Christianity dressed up in the language of reason and world-improvement. Conrad's was a more austere view, a modern renewal of the ancient pagan sense of fate that is given voice in Greek tragedy.

The political religions of the twentieth century were at one in rejecting the idea that history is fated. Marxism and market liberalism both promised a time when its tragedies could be left behind. Both saw history as a process of progressive emancipation ending in a universal civilization. Both believed that, with the growth of knowledge, all of humanity would come to share the same values. This is the Enlightenment faith in progress that Conrad rejected. Nowadays, our thinking made lax by a constant emphasis on feeling, we imagine that the idea of progress expresses an attitude of optimism, and its rejection pessimism. In fact, the idea of progress does more than express an attitude: it embodies a theory – one that has never had much to support it, and which was falsified in the century that has just ended.

The core of the belief in progress is that human values and goals converge in parallel with our increasing knowledge. The twentieth century shows the contrary. Human beings use the power of scientific knowledge to assert and defend the values and goals they already have. New technologies can be used to alleviate suffering and enhance freedom. They can, and will, also be used to wage war and strengthen tyranny. Science made possible the technologies that powered the industrial revolution. In the twentieth century, these technologies were used to implement state terror and genocide on an unprecedented scale. Ethics and politics do not advance in line with the growth of knowledge – not even in the long run.

It is no accident that nothing approaching a great political novel appeared in the last decades of the twentieth century. The shallow orthodoxies of the time were not propitious. Not only the right, but also the centre left, had made a sacred fetish of science – not, as in *The Secret Agent*, the science of astronomy, but the rather shakier discipline of economics. Practically every part of the political spectrum accepted the ridiculous notion that the secret of unending prosperity had been found. Free markets, balanced budgets, the correct supply of the correctly measured money, a judicious modicum of state spending – with such modest devices, the riddle of history had at last been solved.

The savants who announced the end of history took for granted that the globalization of markets would lead to peace. They did not notice that savage wars were being fought in many parts of the world. The economists who bored on about a weightless economy, which had dispensed with the need for natural resources, contrived to pass over the twentieth century's last big military conflict, the Gulf war, which was fought to protect oil supplies. None of this mattered much so long as the boom continued, and the illusion of peace was preserved. Yet the price of living on these fictions was a hollowing-out not only of politics, but also of literature. It is a telling fact about the closing decades of the twentieth century that the closest approximation to a notable political novel was probably *The Bonfire of the Vanities*.

Conrad is our contemporary because, almost alone among nineteenth- and twentieth-century novelists, he writes of the realities in which we live. At bottom, we know the dilemmas we face are not wholly soluble; but we prefer not to dwell on that. In order to avoid ethnic and religious enmities interacting with the rising scarcity of oil, water and other necessities, we need a worldwide programme of restraint and conservation; but such a programme is difficult to imagine at the best of times, and impossible while crucial regions of the world are at war. The realistic prospect is that the most we can do is stave off disaster, a task that demands stoicism and fortitude, not the utopian imagination. Which other novelist can school us so well in these forgotten virtues?

Conrad's greatness is that he brings us back to our actual life. The callow, rationalistic philosophies of the twentieth century, promising world peace and a universal civilization, are poor guides to a time in which war, terror and empire have returned. It falls to a novelist without much faith in the power of reason to enlighten us how to live reasonably in these circumstances. As to the ideologues of the end of history, prophets of a new world united under the sign of the market, their day is done. It will surely not be long before we find them, like Ossipon, marching in the gutter in the leather yoke of the sandwich board.

April 29, 2002

12

BACK TO HOBBES

In the twentieth century the state was the chief enemy of freedom. Today, it is the weakness of the state that most threatens freedom. In many parts of the world, states have collapsed. In others, the state is corroded or corrupt. The result is that billions of people lack the most rudimentary conditions of a decent life. Even in many rich countries fear of crime is pervasive. Yet liberals – mesmerized by the terrible record of state-sponsored crimes against humanity – continue to believe that the main challenge of politics is to limit state power. Believing there are human freedoms that must never be violated, they insist that everything governments do be consistent with human rights.

The trouble with this simple-minded liberal philosophy is that it treats freedom as a natural condition that develops spontaneously as soon as government repression is removed. In fact, freedom is an extremely complicated and delicate construction that can be maintained only by making continuous adjustments. Contrary to the legalistic strain of liberalism that is currently dominant, liberty is not a system of interlocking rights that must be maintained come what may. One freedom can undermine another. Politics is the art of choosing between rival freedoms.

In the make-believe world of liberal philosophers, we do not have to choose which of our liberties we value the most. In a well-ordered constitution, we can have them all. Such is the constantly reiterated view of American liberal legalists such as John Rawls and Ronald Dworkin. In the real world, things are done rather differently. When legal niceties were tossed aside in the United States and suspects rounded up and secretly interned after the terrorist attacks, liberals were shocked. Yet the American response was entirely predictable. That is what always happens when there is a serious threat to peace. No doubt the Bush administration's actions were in some respects ill-considered and excessive. Even so, it cannot be criticized simply for departing from a strict regard for personal freedom.

At bottom, the state exists to secure peace. Whenever peace is at odds with liberty, it is always liberty that loses out. As Hobbes knew, what human beings want most from the state is not freedom but protection. This may be regrettable, but building a political philosophy on the denial of human nature is foolish. It is better to face facts. Personal liberties do not naturally dovetail. Often they make competing demands, and when they do, the task of government is to craft a mix that affords citizens an acceptable degree of security.

At present, although the actions of governments often belie their words, political discourse is still fixated on fear of the state. Its thinking still addled by cranky libertarian ideas, the right harps on about the virtues of small government. The centre left recognizes that size is not the issue, but insists that government must be bound by individual rights in everything it does.

What both the right and left have not understood is that if it is to provide the security its citizens demand, government should be highly invasive in some contexts and withdraw almost entirely from others. Curbs on liberty that are right in some contexts may be wrong in others. In order to protect its citizens, the state may have to subject them to high levels of surveillance. At the same time, it should stop trying to regulate people's lives where doing so is counter-productive and damaging to society.

Current attitudes to drugs and terrorism illustrate the flaws in the prevailing thinking about the state. Governments tell us that the war on drugs and the war on terrorism go hand in hand, and accordingly demand draconian powers to prosecute them. Liberals are suspicious of the rhetoric of war, and insist that governments must in both cases be bound by a regime of rights. Neither side recognizes that whereas dealing with terrorism may demand an enhancement of the state's powers, coping with drug use requires a far less invasive state.

The case for legalizing drugs is usually stated in terms that hark back to the 1960s: individuals should be left alone when what they are doing affects no one but themselves. This formula echoes John Stuart Mill's celebrated dictum that in the part of his conduct that concerns only himself, the individual is sovereign. Mill's principle would not justify legalization today. Particularly when it leads to health problems, drug use cannot avoid affecting other people. Moreover, the range of drugs consumed is vastly larger now than it was in Mill's day. Drugs – legal and illegal – are products of worldwide industries whose activities have far-reaching effects on society and the economy. In these circumstances, it is silly to think that drug use falls into the category of a purely private activity.

The case for legalizing drugs has very little directly to do with personal freedom. Certainly, it does not depend on the idea that drugs affect only their users. On the contrary, it is precisely because they affect society at large that their use should be legalized. Government should confine itself to education, regulating quality and providing treatment for people whose drug use has become problematic. Prohibiting drugs has led to far more casualties than drug use itself.

The first casualty of a regime of prohibition is public health. When drugs are illegal, their quality cannot be controlled. When they are used intravenously, they spread dangerous or deadly diseases such as hepatitis and HIV. A second casualty is crime control. Wherever drugs are prohibited, their price rises steeply, leading to high levels of crime on the part of users. Conversely, the profits of the illegal drugs trade are huge. As a result, criminal organizations are able to bribe the police and, in some countries, to co-opt governments. That leads on to a third casualty – global security. All over the world, terrorist organizations get a sizeable portion of their funds from the illegal drugs trade. Arguably, terrorists are the single greatest beneficiaries from the current prohibitionist regime.

Though liberals are reluctant to admit it, what is loosely called terrorism is actually a new kind of unconventional war, one that has arisen from the weakness of state power in many parts of the world. We are used to thinking of war as a form of conflict among states. That may have been largely true during much of the modern period, but it is worth noting that, over the past decade or so, war has ceased to be chiefly a conflict between states. The Falklands war and the Gulf war were armed encounters between states, but in the Balkans,

Afghanistan and, more recently, the Middle East, war has followed a different pattern.

In each case, some of the protagonists are not states, but political organizations or fundamentalist networks over which no state has much leverage. Al-Qaeda is one such network. Governments like to talk about defeating or eradicating terrorism, but in fact the task of controlling such groups is open-ended and dauntingly difficult.

One reason why the Bush administration's obsession with securing a change of regime in Iraq is so badly misguided is that it will do little to hamper the activities of terrorists, and, by further alienating the Arab world, may end up making the job of containing them harder. There is a deeper flaw in this thinking: where there has been nothing resembling a modern state for some time, as in Afghanistan, the use of force can achieve only very limited ends. This is even more clearly true in Iraq, where the state could well break up in the aftermath of a US attack. Whether or not it can be morally justified, waging war in these circumstances is futile unless it is followed by a long period of state-building.

At least in America, official thinking does not accept the need to renovate the state in countries where it is weak. Unfortunately, liberal thinkers contribute to this intellectual default by identifying states as the principal violators of human rights. That may have been true during much of the twentieth century. Only a modern state could have perpetrated the Holocaust or established the Gulag. The world still contains many highly repressive states. Nevertheless, the risks most potentially catastrophic to human rights no longer emanate from states. The last big genocide of the century, in Rwanda, was the work not of a state, but of irregular ethnic militias. Equally, the current threat from weapons of mass destruction is not that states will use them, but that they may leak out of the control of states. Today, weak states pose a greater danger to human freedom than tyrants.

Liberals refuse to accept this. They are adamant that the dangers arising from terrorism cannot justify new restrictions on liberty. Rightly, they point to the fact that once governments acquire such powers, they rarely give them up. Certainly David Blunkett's proposals for monitoring communications were absurdly sweeping. But are we really unwilling to give up any of our freedoms, if that is the price of reducing the risks of catastrophe?

From Locke to Mill, Kant to Rawls, liberal thinkers have tried to put the state in a straitjacket. In our time, Hobbes may be a better guide than any of these worthies. He cannot tell us how to deal with enemies of freedom who do not fear death; but at least he understood that freedom is not the normal human condition. It is an artefact of state power. If you want to be free, you need first to be safe. For that, you need a strong state. Hobbes understood this because he lived in a period of civil war. Let's hope we do not have to suffer something similar – or worse – before we stop demonizing the state.

August 19, 2002

13

THE NEW WARS OF SCARCITY

The outlines of the world in which we will live over the coming century have become clearer. The end of secular ideology has not brought peace. It has simply changed the character of war. In the Persian Gulf and central Asia, in Africa and the South China Sea, we see nations playing out new struggles. Those struggles are about the control of scarce resources. Ideological conflicts are being replaced by geopolitics. The strategic rivalries of the cold war are being followed by resource wars.

This, in many ways, is a return to normalcy. The ideological struggles of the twentieth century were extremely anomalous. Throughout history, wars have been fought over gold and silver, access to rivers and fertile land. If we find the emergent pattern of conflict unfamiliar, it is because we are still haunted by nineteenth-century utopian visions in which the spread of industry throughout the world ushers in an age of perpetual peace.

Until mid-Victorian times, most thinkers regarded scarcity in the necessities of life as the natural human condition. They agreed with Malthus that there are limits to growth – particularly in human numbers. The earth's resources are finite; they cannot be stretched to accommodate the unlimited wants of an exponentially growing human population. As John Stuart Mill argued, this does not mean there is no prospect of improving the quality of human life. New inventions can bring a comfortable and leisurely existence to increasing numbers of people, so long as overall human numbers are themselves kept in check. Human progress cannot transgress the limits imposed by natural scarcity.

With the accelerating advance of the industrial revolution, this insight was lost. With few exceptions, the great economists and social theorists of the late nineteenth and early twentieth centuries believed that, with the rise of industrialism, scarcity could be overcome. Marx and Keynes disagreed on many fundamental points, but they were one in believing that in modern industrial economies natural resources are basically irrelevant. If Marx envisioned a world in which goods had become so abundant that they need not have a price, Keynes was not far behind in declaring that mankind's economic problems had been solved.

Towards the end of the twentieth century, Hayek voiced a similar view when he insisted that in a world ruled by the free market there were no insuperable limits to economic growth. This fantasy has become part of the conventional wisdom of all mainstream parties, whose leaders continue to recite the Nineties mantra that we live in weightless economies that are decreasingly dependent on the limited resources of the earth.

The belief that resource scarcity can be transcended by industrialism unites many seemingly antagonistic political standpoints. When neo-liberals announced that the collapse of communism meant the end of history, they showed how much they have in common with their Marxist opponents. They assumed that once the struggle of capitalism with central planning had ended, so would geopolitical conflict. In the global free market, as in Marx's vision of world communism, there would be no shortage of the necessities of life.

It did not occur to these breathless missionaries of the free market that worldwide industrialization might trigger a new and dangerous kind of conflict. Like Marx, they took it for granted that wars of scarcity are relics of the pre-industrial past.

Yet the neo-liberals, unlike Marx, had a clear example of a resource war waged by an advanced industrial society right under their noses. Even more clearly than the likely war in Iraq, the Gulf war was fought to retain control of western energy supplies. If Saddam had been allowed to take Kuwait, he would have controlled a crucial part of the world's oil reserves. There is plenty of oil left in the world; but most of it is much more expensive to extract than the oil that lies in the regions around Iraq and Kuwait. The Persian Gulf contains the world's last great pool of cheap conventional oil. Any protracted disruption of supply or price increase in this vital resource would be disastrous for advanced industrial countries such as the US and Japan. This economic vulnerability, and not the threat posed by radical Islam, is the chief reason why the Gulf is the focus of global conflict.

That does not mean the threat of radical Islam is unreal or insignificant, but rather that it is mostly indirect. Whatever Osama Bin Laden may now say, al-Qaeda's strategic goals are regional, not global. Its central aim has always been to topple the House of Saud. To be sure, achieving that objective has embroiled it in a global struggle against US power. As things

stand, Saudi Arabia, the most important of the Gulf producers, supplies oil to the west in return for American protection.
It is implicit in the logic of this situation that al-Qaeda and the
US should be deadly enemies. Even so, the threat posed by al-
Qaeda does not come from its demonstrated ability to mount
terrorist operations in the west. It comes from the fragility of
the Saudi regime.

Saudi Arabia is almost entirely dependent on oil for its
income. In addition – and here the Reverend Malthus makes
an appearance – it has a population that is expected to double
in roughly 20 years. (In this it is no different from other countries in the region.) The combination of high population
growth with near-complete reliance on a single depleting commodity is not a recipe for political stability. Largely because of
population growth, the country's per capita income has fallen
by between a half and three-quarters since the early 1980s. If
this decline continues over the next 20 years, a certainty unless
the price of oil rises substantially, the result can only be severe
economic and political strain.

Radical Islam is well placed to benefit. Heavily subsidized
through the Saudi education system, it stands to recruit millions of unemployed and displaced young males as the
economy deteriorates. The demographic explosion, combined
with falling incomes and the advancing power of Islamic fundamentalism, makes the Saudi regime inherently unstable. It is
a bold forecaster who predicts that it will be in existence a
decade from now.

For some members of the Bush administration, the weakness of the Saudi regime is a reason for trying to reshape it in
a way that better suits US interests and values. These strategists
do not confine their designs to Saudi Arabia. They aim to

engineer regime changes throughout the region. Their policies cannot be explained entirely in geopolitical terms. As is often the case in US foreign policy, they contain an incongruous element of idealism.

American policy-makers who support regime changes across much of the Middle East genuinely believe that democratic regimes installed on the back of American military power will be more popularly legitimate than indigenous tyrannies. In this, they are dangerously deluded. In a region where American power attracts implacable hatred, any attempt at political engineering by the US can only inflame anti-American feeling. The larger risk is that it will boost support for al-Qaeda and other radical Islamic groups to the point of triggering uncontrollable upheaval in several countries. In that event, America's geopolitical interests in the region will be among the casualties.

It is natural to focus on the Gulf when thinking of the role of oil in global conflict, but it is only one piece of the geopolitical jigsaw. In central Asia, the great powers – the US, Russia and China – have re-started the Great Game. No doubt the sudden rapprochement that blossomed between Russia and America after the attacks of 11 September was partly to do with the need for greater co-operation in counter-terrorist strategies, but its deeper rationale has to do with the belief in the Bush administration that the US must diversify its energy supplies. Well before al-Qaeda's attacks, American planners were considering changes in policy aimed at diminishing US reliance on Gulf oil. The prize that Bush seeks in his dealings with Vladimir Putin is secure access to the natural riches of the Caspian Basin. A similar imperative underpins America's renewed interest in Africa, where large oil reserves have been found.

Beyond the current turmoil in the Gulf, still larger conflicts are shaping up. It would be wrong to think that the return of geopolitics results chiefly from flaws in US policy. It is an integral feature of industrialization worldwide. You can catch a glimpse of the future in the struggles that are emerging around the South China Sea. Stretching from Taiwan and China to the Philippines, Indonesia, Malaysia and Vietnam, this is an area rich in undersea resources, particularly oil and natural gas. Competition for this natural wealth has triggered many bitter maritime disputes, in which the protagonists seem fully prepared to use military force. As a result, it is the site of an intensifying regional arms race.

The conflicts in the South China Sea are important chiefly in what they portend for the future. As Asia industrializes, its energy needs will rise steeply. Inevitably, Asian countries will find themselves in competition, with each other and with the west – for scarce reserves of hydrocarbons. It may be this prospect that underlies the conviction of some American military strategists that the long-term threat to US security comes not from radical Islam but from China. How will this vast country supply its energy needs when it is fully industrialized? If it comes into competition with the US for the world's remaining reserves of oil and natural gas, can there be any assurance that the conflict will not escalate into war?

If the twenty-first century looks set to be punctuated by resource wars, the reason is not that a few countries – the US now, China in the future – are greedily seizing the wealth of the planet. The logic of resource war is deeper. Intensifying competition for natural resources flows inexorably from worldwide industrialization – a process that is seen by practically everyone today as enabling humanity to emancipate itself from scarcity. In fact, industrialization creates a new set of scarcities.

The continued growth in human population increases strain on the environment, not least on the habitats of other species. The pressure is enhanced when this growing population demands an industrial lifestyle that has hitherto been confined to a few. The combined impact of population growth and industrialization is producing environmental changes on a scale unprecedented in history. In parts of the world, fresh water is becoming a non-renewable resource. Globally, climate change is altering living conditions drastically for billions of people. In these circumstances, it is difficult not to see the Gulf war and war in Iraq as precursors of other and perhaps larger conflicts.

Military planners in many countries accept that the risk of resource wars is serious and increasing, but it continues to be denied by economists and avoided by politicians. In the case of politicians, the reason is clear: voters have little appetite for bad news. With economists, particularly those of the sectarian neo-liberal variety, denial of the reality of resource wars has more complex sources. Like Marx, they believe that, given the right economic system, technology can rid humankind of the imme-morial evils of scarcity and war. For Marxists, the best system is socialism; for neo-liberals, the free market. What ideologues of both camps possess is the faith – and it is faith, not a result of any rational inquiry – that technology will allow human beings to make a break with history and create a new world.

The trouble with the cult of technology is not that it exag-gerates the power that comes with the practical application of scientific knowledge. It is that it forgets the unregenerate human beings who use it. Developments in genetics may allow the eradication of inherited defects that produce painful or disabling diseases; but they also allow for the creation of genetically selective bio-weapons. New types of energy may be invented which greatly reduce the role of hydrocarbons in industrial economies. If so, we can be sure they will soon be turned to military uses.

It may be true that in a much better economic system, new technologies could spin out natural resources endlessly. I very much doubt that this is possible, if only because the laws of thermodynamics seem to rule out perpetual motion machines. But even if a world without scarcity were technically feasible, it would remain humanly impossible. Historic human conflicts would prevent it from ever coming into being.

The neo-liberals who greeted the collapse of communism as the end of history made a monumental error. This was partly because, blinded by simple-minded economic formulae, they failed to take account of certain rather familiar facts of geography and history. Natural resources are not spread equally around the world. They are distributed unevenly, often in regions wracked by long-standing conflicts. This is most obviously true of oil: America's geopolitical strategy in the Gulf could further aggravate the region's intractable divisions. In the South China Sea, too, rival claims over coastal resources inflame historic enmities.

It is not only neo-liberals who failed to anticipate the return of geopolitics. Blinded by a naïve faith in technology, few people have yet perceived the ironies of history that are unfolding before our eyes. In using their technology to assert control of natural resources, the world's most advanced economies show that they remain dependent on the finite and fragile earth for their prosperity and even their existence. At the same time, they are being drawn into ancient wars of religion and ethnicity. As might have been foreseen, the new era of perpetual peace that was announced just a few years ago has turned out to be a high-tech rerun of the most old-fashioned conflicts.

November 25, 2002

14

AMERICA'S WAR ON EVIL

According to Javier Solana, formerly secretary general of Nato and currently the European Union's high representative for foreign relations and security, US foreign policy, particularly towards terrorism, is increasingly shaped by a belief in evil. In Europe, we see terrorism as one of several threats to the world. They include poverty and climate change, and each has causes that can be alleviated. In America, by contrast, terrorism is seen as supremely evil, the work of dark forces that must be defeated and eliminated. This rift in transatlantic attitudes is not simply a reflection of diverging interests and priorities. It is a difference in worldview. The perception of evil that drives current American foreign policy makes sense against the background of the intense religiosity that pervades American culture. It is only in this context that one can represent Saddam Hussein or the Palestine Liberation Organization as expressions of sheer malignity. In secular, post-Christian Europe, Solana seems to be suggesting, we simply do not believe in evil in this way.

Solana cannot be accused of venting anti-American prejudices. He is a lifelong Atlanticist, whose account of American policy is extremely well informed and squares with many of the signals emanating from Washington. Not only the in-famous 'axis of evil' speech, with its lumping together of quite different regimes into a single category of all-round turpitude, but also many other public statements indicate that powerful elements in the White House see the international system in terms of a stark conflict of good and evil.

In itself this is nothing new. Dividing the world into goodies and baddies is a recurrent feature of American thinking. President Ronald Reagan denounced the Soviet Union as an 'evil empire' in the 1980s. Much earlier in the twentieth century, a similar view underpinned President Woodrow Wilson's belief that Europe's only salvation was in remaking itself on an American model of national self-determination. Today, the idea that the US embodies all that is good in the world is an article of faith in the 'new strategic doctrine' presented to the US Congress in September 2002, in which President Bush declared that there is 'a single sustainable model for national success': American democracy and free enterprise. This Wilsonian faith in universal democracy owes something to the European Enlightenment, but it is at bottom an indigenously American creed, rooted in the belief that the United States has been chosen by God to bring freedom and virtue into a benighted world.

With their repeated experience of devastating war, Europeans are rightly suspicious of attempts to turn diplo-macy into a moral crusade. Solana deserves credit for speaking candidly about a transatlantic cultural divide that widens by the day. Even so, it seems to me that his analysis of US foreign policy is in one crucial respect misleading. The implication is that Americans believe in evil and Europeans do not. It is a diagnosis that US neo-conservatives, who delight in portraying Europeans as shifty, morally relativistic wimps, will heartily endorse. In fact the opposite is true. It is disbelief in evil that is today peculiarly American.

After an encounter with a well-meaning American who believed that war could be abolished for ever if only international relations were in the hands of reasonable men, Jean-Paul Sartre declared: 'I believe in the existence of evil and he does not.' Sartre captured the real difference between American and European world-views. For all its unremitting piety, American culture is far removed from the traditional Christian doctrine that human life is marked indelibly by sin. Rather, American culture is animated by what has always been seen as a heresy – Pelagius' doctrine that human nature is not inherently flawed but instead essentially good. Contrary to a venerable academic cliché, American culture is not Manichean. True, the Manicheans – followers of a third-century Persian religious teacher – were radical dualists who divided the world into the forces of darkness and light; but they believed good and evil to be coeval, and the struggle between them unending. In contrast, contemporary American culture is founded on the Pelagian faith that evil can be defeated and eradicated from the world.

Born somewhere in Celtic Britain in the middle of the fourth century, Pelagius was a theologian who achieved fame by attacking the teaching of St Augustine, according to which evil is an intrinsic part of human nature. For Augustine, humans can and should strive for the good; but they can never fully realize it. Society and government will always be radically imperfect. Rejecting this eminently sensible Augustinian view, Pelagius initiated a tradition of thought that eventually gave birth to modern humanism.

When George W Bush uses the language of evil to describe the international system, he is doing more than transpose theological categories into the always morally ambivalent realm of diplomacy and war, where they plainly do not belong. He is endorsing the heretical belief that evil can be banished from the world by an act of human will. Bush is inordinately fond of talking up the threat posed to the world by evil forces; but he evinces not the slightest doubt that, given the right kind of moral resoluteness, they can be wholly destroyed. Far from being grounded in the Christian insight that humans have an ingrained predilection for evil, he is driven by a militant version of the Pelagian faith that human will can eradicate the evils we find in the world. In contrast, Europeans see the choices that have to be made in international relations as being unavoidably among evils. Long experience has taught them that in dangerous conflicts the best intentions can have the most horrific results. No doubt they continue to hope for a better world, but they are always conscious of the danger of too much enthusiasm. Even where Europeans seem entirely secular in outlook, history has made most of them instinctive Augustinians.

The danger of American foreign policy is not that it is obsessed with evil but that it is based on the belief that evil can be abolished. It is a conviction the British Prime Minister seems to share. Pledging support for the American 'war on terror', Tony Blair declared: 'We will not rest until this evil is driven from our world.' Few diplomats or military men share his view that evil can be eradicated.

History suggests that opposing terrorism is a long haul in which peace can never be taken for granted. In Northern Ireland, a counter-terrorist campaign, which involved peace moves as well as security measures, has been in operation for decades. It has finally brought the chief protagonists into the political process; but terrorism has still not disappeared. The same is true in the Basque country. In neither case has the counter-terrorist strategy failed. On the contrary, it has succeeded: the threat has been subdued, contained and reduced to more tolerable levels.

The risks of imagining that evil can be conjured away are many, and they are nowhere more evident than in US policy on Iraq. With overwhelming force at their disposal, the confidence of American military planners that the present Iraqi regime can be destroyed without much difficulty may prove to be justified; but the bland optimism of America's civilian leadership regarding the costs and risks of reconstructing Iraq in the aftermath of war is desperately deluded. Even if it is quickly over, war will exact a terrible human price. Many thousands of people will be killed, hundreds of thousands subjected to extremes of suffering. Refugees could run into millions. These are not conditions conducive to a swift transition to stable democratic government, particularly in a state that has disparate ethnic and religious groupings, some of which have been deadly enemies in the recent past. A long period of occupation may be required. After all, UN forces have been in Cyprus for nearly 40 years, containing a nasty but far less dangerous conflict than we are likely to see in Iraq. Yet the White House talks of an occupation of Iraq lasting a mere 18 months.

This assessment exemplifies a more far-reaching lack of realism in US thinking. For the pro-war faction that seems to have prevailed in the internecine struggles of the Bush administration, toppling Saddam Hussein is only the first move in reshaping much of the Middle East. Not only Iraq, but also Saudi Arabia, Iran and a number of other countries appear to be candidates for 'regime change'. Tyranny is to be overthrown and democracy installed throughout the region. From one angle, this grandiose scheme is a rerun of Woodrow Wilson's plans for central and eastern Europe in the aftermath of the First World War. Wilson's dream of national self-determination foundered in the bloody realities of ethnic nationalism. If the US attempts anything similar in the Middle East the result can only be the same, if not worse. American power is hated implacably throughout the region. Indigenous tyrannies are likely to prove more popularly legitimate than US-backed democracies.

The knock-on effect of US military occupation of Iraq is unlikely to end in the Gulf. It could well be felt as far away as Pakistan, which could become the first failed state with nuclear capability, and in Indonesia, the world's most populous Muslim country. To be sure, these are risks and not certainties; but they must be put in the reckoning along with the undoubted evil of war. The option of simply choosing the good does not exist.

It is true that, if the US does not go to war, great evil may also result. Saddam may get his hands on nuclear weapons; the Middle East could become the site of a nuclear arms race. On the other hand, the invasion of Iraq may not go as smoothly as planned. If Saddam attacks US forces or Israel with chemical or biological weapons, can we be sure that nuclear weapons will not be used in response? So far, despite proliferation to Stalinist Russia and to Maoist China, deterrence has worked. Nuclear weapons have not been used since the bombing of

Hiroshima and Nagasaki. Will the world be better if they are deployed as part of an attempt to block their acquisition by an unpalatable regime?

The relentlessly upbeat moral outlook that underpins American foreign policy prevents a clear assessment of these risks, because it forbids us from admitting that in international relations we are commonly faced with choices among evils. It also inhibits honesty about more mundane interests, such as secure oil supplies and Bush's re-election prospects. The belief that evil can be driven from the world nourishes a false sense of moral purity. US policy, like that of any imperial power, is dictated largely by realpolitik. Morality, though it may constrain foreign policy, can never be the chief force in shaping it. This is a hard truth, but one long known to Augustinians. The result of denying it is that even when genuine moral concern appears in international affairs it is treated with cynicism.

America's critics condemn Bush's call to take up arms against evil as an expression of religious fundamentalism. And it is true that fundamentalism has an alarming hold on US government. But if Bush talks so insistently of evil, it is because he belongs in a tradition of American piety that does not finally believe in it. Like Woodrow Wilson before him, he does not doubt that once the world has accepted American values, it will enjoy everlasting peace and prosperity. This has not always been the American view of things. For the founding fathers, human beings were flawed creatures that no change in institutions could improve fundamentally. The purpose of government was not to conduct us to the Promised Land but to stave off the recurrent evils to which human life is naturally prone.

Today, this sane and realistic viewpoint is rare and politics is ruled by an unforgiving moral optimism. This is a curious state of affairs, as the truth of human imperfectibility that is preserved in religious myth has been confirmed in the most advanced reaches of modern thought. Freud and sociobiology are at one in setting definite limits to the possibilities of human progress. Without endorsing any theistic narrative of the fall of man, they vindicate the truth in the doctrine of original sin. The revival of the language of evil in the speeches of American leaders does not mean that this ancient truth has been rediscovered. On the contrary, it is a sign that we are in for another grandiose experiment in remaking the world, with all the farce and horror that invariably entails.

January 20, 2003

15

TORTURE: A MODEST PROPOSAL

A new phase in the evolution of liberal values is under way in the United States. America's most celebrated defender of civil liberties has initiated a new debate on torture. The context of Professor Alan Dershowitz's argument is American, but its meaning, like that of all true liberal principles, is universal. The force of his argument promises to transform liberal institutions throughout the world.

Using impeccable scholarship and the most rigorous logic, the distinguished Harvard legal scholar has demonstrated that nothing in the US Constitution forbids the use of torture. In interviews with the American media, Dershowitz has noted that while the Fifth Amendment prohibits self-incrimination, that means only that statements elicited by torture cannot be used as evidence against the person who has been tortured. It does not prohibit torture itself. Neither does the Eighth Amendment, since the ban on 'cruel and unusual punishments' applies only after an individual has been convicted. The belief that torture is unconstitutional in America may be widespread, but it is a fallacy, the product of rudimentary errors in legal reasoning.

Torture is permitted by the American Constitution, but it

remains legally unregulated. To fill this gap, Dershowitz advocates the introduction of 'torture warrants'. Just as the FBI applies to the courts for search warrants, so it should be able to apply for torture warrants. At present, there is nothing in the law that explicitly authorizes the use of torture to extract information from terrorists. If it is used, as it often is, it is used extra-legally. As Dershowitz has pointed out, this is a highly unsatisfactory state of affairs. The rule of law is a core liberal value. It cannot be compromised in the fight against terrorism. Torture, therefore, must cease to be something practised beyond the law; it must become part of normal judicial procedure.

If liberal thinkers in the past have shied away from rigorous thinking about torture, it is because they have been unduly influenced by history. Enlightenment thinkers such as Montesquieu and Voltaire campaigned indefatigably against judicial torture, and viewed its abolition as a vital step in human progress. In their own time, no doubt, they were right. These partisans of liberty were locked in conflict with the entrenched tyrannies of Europe's *ancien régime*. In attacking judicial torture, they were aligning themselves with the cause of progress and humanity.

The present situation is quite different. In the despotic, reactionary states against which Montesquieu and Voltaire struggled, torture was used to bolster arbitrary power. Now the liberal civilization of which they dreamt actually exists – in the United States of America. Today torture is used to defend free societies from attack by their enemies. Many liberals, especially in Europe, seem unable to grasp this elementary distinction. Mired in the past, they are blind to the emerging new regime of universal rights.

Where European thinkers have allowed recourse to torture at all, they have allowed it only in extreme situations. For Hobbes, justice was a set of conventions that societies adopted in order to achieve what he called 'commodious living', a peaceful, civilized existence. When order breaks down, in this view, the conventions of justice lapse. If a radiological bomb has been planted on the London Underground, torture may be the only way of disarming the device in time and thereby saving hundreds of thousands of lives. No government can avoid recourse to torture in such circumstances. Human beings turn to the state for security. If the state fails to provide it, it will be overthrown.

The trouble with this view of torture is that it remains stuck in the blood-soaked history of old Europe. It assumes that any act of torture leaves an indelible moral stain, even when the alternative, the destruction of many innocent lives, is unthinkable. It reduces torture to a desperate expedient whose rightful place, if it has one, is in darkened cellars. Seeing the struggle against terrorism in this way only weakens our resolve. Rather than wallowing in pessimism, we need to view the reintroduction of judicial torture as the next step in human progress.

Bringing torture out of the cellar into the clear light of day will require a far-reaching modernization of the law, but before that can be achieved we need a parallel reform in our thinking about human rights. Fortunately, we can draw on the most advanced thinking in contemporary liberal philosophy, the theory of justice elaborated by the late John Rawls. The eminent Harvard philosopher seems not to have grasped the full implications of his theory; but one of its central features is the insight that basic liberties cannot conflict. For European thinkers such as Hobbes and John Stuart Mill, one liberty collides with another; and the same freedom exercised by one person can conflict with that of another. Freedom of expression clashes with freedom from hate speech; one person's freedom of association (in a whites-only club, for example) is another's wrongful discrimination. Hobbes and Mill saw these as conflicts that we cannot hope to resolve completely; the best we can do is to strive for a compromise in which the competing claims are balanced against one another.

American liberal philosophers have rejected this messy and uninspiring view. They have shown that all our liberties belong in a single, unified system. When they are properly 'contoured' – that is, defined so that they cannot collide with one another – human rights need never conflict. Thus, when freedom of speech clashes with freedom from hate speech, it is denied that the latter is a genuine freedom.

The relevance of this insight to the question of torture should be self-evident. The belief that torture is always wrong is a prejudice inherited from an obsolete philosophy. We need to shed the belief that human rights are violated when a terrorist is tortured. As Rawls and others have shown, basic freedoms must form a coherent whole. Self-evidently, there can be no right to attack basic human rights. Therefore, once the proper legal procedures are in place, torturing terrorists cannot violate their rights. In fact, in a truly liberal society, terrorists have an inalienable right to be tortured.

This is what demonstrates the moral superiority of liberal societies over others, past and present. Other societies have degraded terrorists by subjecting them to lawless and unaccountable power. In the new world that is taking shape, terrorists, although they themselves degrade human rights by practising terrorism, will be afforded the full dignity of due legal process, even while being tortured. We can look forward to a time when this right will be available universally.

It is clear that the new regime of human rights that is emerging will not be confined to the United States. The US will not rest until other states have also adopted it. Developing a modern, liberal regime for the practice of torture will require reform of international treaties. The UN Declaration of Universal Human Rights embodies the discredited view that torture is inherently incompatible with respect for human rights. Along with other international treaties, it needs modernization. Securing agreement on the changes that are required may seem a daunting task. Our experience during the Iraq crisis suggests it is not impossible, however. Using its formidable resources, the US has persuaded a number of refractory states of the wisdom of launching a pre-emptive attack to dislodge the rights-violating regime of Saddam Hussein. It can surely be relied upon to secure a similar agreement around reform of the international law on torture.

There is a deeper reason for believing that the new regime of rights will be universal. Dershowitz's contention that torture is not forbidden by the US Constitution may look like a purely local argument; but that is to disregard the universal validity of the principles on which the Constitution is founded. Human rights are not just cultural or legal constructions, as fashionable western relativists are fond of claiming. They are universal values. To deny the benefits of the new regime of rights to other cultures is to patronize them in a way that is reminiscent of the colonial era. If the new regime on torture is good enough for the US, who can say that it is not good for everyone?

In practice, there will be countries that resist the new order and refuse to reintroduce torture. Such rogue states are nothing new. Those that choose to defy the emerging consensus, however, must accept that they thereby place their legitimacy in question. States that refuse to modernize their laws on torture cannot expect the protection afforded them in the past by old-fashioned notions of sovereignty. They must expect increasing pressure to conform to global norms. If, despite all attempts at persuasion, they persist in opposing the international community, they will face action to enforce regime change.

No one will deny that the reintroduction of torture into the legal process will present some tricky problems. At present, torture is normally contracted out to less developed countries; but sending terrorists to friendly dictatorships for interrogation is hypocritical, and possibly inefficient. Surely it is far better that we do the job ourselves. If we do, however, we will need a trained body of interrogators, backed up by a staff of doctors, psychiatrists and other specialists. A new breed of lawyer will have to deal with the cases that are bound to arise when people suffer injury or death under interrogation. We shall need expert social workers, trained to help the families of subjects under interrogation. Universities in particular must show they are capable of delivering the skills that will be required.

It would be wrong to forget the needs of the interrogators themselves. In the past, torturers were shunned as outcasts, a tacit admission that they acted as the servants of tyrants. If we are to put interrogators to work in defence of liberal values, their role in the community must receive proper recognition. They will require intensive counselling to overcome the inevitable traumas that this difficult work involves. They must be enabled to see themselves as dedicated workers in the cause of progress. Psychotherapy must be available to help them avoid the negative self-image from which some torturers have suffered in the past. Unlike torturers who violated human rights at the behest of tyrants, interrogators who apply their skills to terrorists today are in the vanguard of human progress. In effect, they are practitioners of a new profession. Those who enter it must feel that society values them.

Changing the law on torture may seem to be only one more item on the agenda of modernization, part of the ongoing process of law reform in which archaic notions about double jeopardy and trial by jury have already been swept away. Still, the problems posed by changing our policies on torture are undoubtedly more challenging than those we have confronted and overcome in other areas of reform. Especially in Europe, the reforms that are so urgently needed run up against an ingrained conservatism that treats inherited patterns of thought as sacrosanct. It is almost as if Europeans no longer believe in progress.

We need nothing less than a fundamental advance in moral thinking. Liberals have often stressed that we must question the values we inherit from the past. The debate initiated by Alan Dershowitz shows that, in America at least, they are not afraid to apply this lesson. The world's finest liberal thinkers are applying themselves to the design of a modern regime of judicial torture. At a time when civilization is under daily threat, there can be no more hopeful sign.

February 17, 2003

16

ON THE EVE OF WAR: AMERICAN POWER AND IMPOTENCE

The approach of war in Iraq has altered the international system irreversibly. Many familiar landmarks will be missing in the new world that is taking shape. Among them could be Tony Blair's premiership, which looks likely to be a casualty of the geopolitical shifts that are now under way.

For the past dozen years, Iraq has been a minor irritant in the system. Although its human costs have been high, the policy of deterrence and containment that has been in force since the first Gulf war has worked well. Saddam may have rattled the bars of his cage from time to time, but the notion that he is a major danger to world peace is laughable. Along with North Korea, Pakistan presents a far greater threat. If a US attack on Iraq produces upheaval in Pakistan, we could be faced with a failed state in which nuclear weapons are no longer under political control. The worst nightmare of anyone worried about the spread of weapons of mass destruction would then be a reality.

Saddam's weapons of mass destruction (if he has any, which he may well do) are a pretext. The decision to invade Iraq was taken many months ago, and the Bush administration is bent on much more than disarmament or even regime change. Its strategic objectives require the occupation of Iraq. The Bush administration has always viewed energy policy as a matter of national security. One of its strategic goals is to end US dependence on oil imports from Saudi Arabia, a regime it sees as colluding with terrorism. In the short to medium term of the next 20 years, the only way this can be done is by acquiring control of Iraq, which contains the world's second-largest pool of cheap oil. That would require a long-term US presence.

Whatever anyone says, therefore, the imminent war is very much about oil. Yet the Bush administration has no realistic idea of how it will secure Iraq's oil; its view of the aftermath of war is muddy in the extreme. Over the past few weeks it has oscillated between talking of rule by an American military governor, on the model of post-war Japan, and promising an immediate transition to democracy. US relations with the Iraqi opposition parties have begun to unravel. There is a risk that the Iraqi state, a rickety structure cobbled together by departing British civil servants, will fracture and fragment in Yugoslav or even Chechen fashion. Some months ago, a swift move by the United Nations may have been feasible. It is not so easily envisaged today. Military rule may turn out to be the only solution, but it demands a degree of commitment and a willingness to accept casualties that the US has not demonstrated for decades.

Uncertainty about how to manage the aftermath of war reflects a deeper confusion in the administration's thinking about the future of the Middle East. There may be those in the administration who imagine that the US can take Iraq without unsettling the status quo in much of the rest of the region, but it seems clear they are no longer calling the shots. In a speech in Washington on 26 February 2003, President Bush stated that the aim of war in Iraq was to bring democracy to the Muslim world. Reshaping the Middle East, he then declared, was part of America's mission to rewrite human history.

In most of the world, Bush's mix of realpolitik and evangelical uplift evokes mere contempt. In the Middle East, it augurs disaster. For much of the region, the choice is not between tyranny and freedom; it is between theocratic democracy and secular dictatorship. Democratic elections in a country such as Saudi Arabia would not bring about the triumph of 'western values', as some members of the Bush administration fondly imagine. As in Algeria, they would result in the political victory of radical Islam. If any country in the region embodies western values, it is Iraq, a thoroughly secular regime. The only Islamic country where secularism has been successfully combined with democracy is Turkey, in which America's effort to pressure the government into support for the war is strengthening Islamist forces.

We have been here before, and the precedent is an ominous one. Current US policy in the Middle East is a replay of the programme of national self-determination that Woodrow Wilson promoted in central and eastern Europe in the wake of the First World War. Now, as then, it has no understanding of the forces it is unleashing: ethnic nationalism then, radical Islam today. The result in the Middle East will be an upheaval as unmanageably destructive as that which shook central Europe in the inter-war period.

The countries of the Middle East face a Malthusian squeeze: their populations will double in roughly 20 years. An attempt to install American-style democracy across a region where US power is already loathed will propel tens of millions of young people, many of them unemployed, into active support for radical Islam. The result can only be terrorism on an even bigger scale.

If Blair continues to maintain that war in Iraq will somehow tame the terrorist threat, the reason is that he has adopted a neo-conservative world-view in which history is on the side of US power. It is often said that, in backing the American attack on Iraq, Blair has proved that he is not the focus-group obsessive he sometimes seems to be, but instead a visionary leader capable of defying popular opinion when he believes he is in the right. Certainly, Blair has the courage that goes with a morally simple view of international relations. Yet I believe that miscalculations led him to his present position, not moral certitude. He misjudged the depth of opposition to the war in Britain and in his own party. He underestimated the difficulties of bringing the UN into line with the US position. He exaggerated the degree to which he could influence the Bush administration against the idea of unilateral action. Above all, he miscalculated US power and the scale of resistance to it.

Like most politicians, Blair has allowed his view of the world to be shaped by the conventional opinion of the past few years – that, with the collapse of communism, we have entered a uni-polar world which will be dominated for the foreseeable future by the US. In this Whiggish philosophy, America not only possesses irresistible power; it embodies human progress.

But conventional opinion, as so often, is wrong. Militarily, the US is in a league of its own but, economically, it is increasingly vulnerable. Unlike Britain during its imperial period, which exported capital throughout the world, the US is the world's greatest debtor. This combination of military might with heavy dependence on foreign capital is bound to under-mine America's ability to pursue a unilateral foreign policy. The first Gulf war was paid for by a coalition that included Germany, Japan and Saudi Arabia. The invasion of Iraq will have to be paid for by the US alone, hence the leaks emanat-ing from the White House suggesting that the cost of occupa-tion will be met by siphoning off some of the revenues from Iraq's oilfields. The US can ill afford its self-appointed role as 'global hegemon'.

If Blair has overestimated US power, he has also misjudged the depth of resistance to it. Conventional opinion has it that France and Russia will not use their power of veto to derail a second UN resolution: they will be brought to heel by a com-bination of bribes and threats to their economies and the damaging impact that unilateral American action would have on the authority of the UN. Maybe so, but in the volatile geopolitical environment that has emerged in the past few weeks, no one can be sure.

For President Jacques Chirac, the use of the veto would rein-force France's position as the dominant European power, and have the added advantage of destroying Blair, the chief spokesman of 'new Europe' within the European Union. At the same time, France's status as a world power would be re-affirmed. It is true that a French veto may trigger a US attack on Iraq and render the UN practically irrelevant so long as Bush remains president; but that may be less permanently damaging than the UN's transformation into an instrument of American unilateralism. If the US finds itself mired in the internecine conflicts of post-war Iraq, France's stance on the war will be triumphantly vindicated.

Anticipating this outcome, President Vladimir Putin of Russia could also decide to use the veto. Faced with these risks, the US may well conclude that enough is enough. Urged on by hawkish advisers who counselled from the start against going the UN route and who view the disastrous political impact on Blair as a bit of collateral damage that the US can live with, Bush could decide to pre-empt a veto and launch an attack before the UN votes. Either way, the uni-polar post-cold war world will be history – and so, I suspect, will be Tony Blair.

Thus, even before it has officially begun, the Iraq war has unravelled the shaky global settlement that was put in place by the Americans in the wake of the cold war. Nato and the EU are more divided than they have ever been; the future of the UN hangs in the balance. As in the nineteenth century, Europe and America are alien civilizations. It is against this background of a changed world that the unprecedented revolt took place in the House of Commons on 26 February. It was not just a vote on the war. It was also an expression of Labour's pent-up fury against the Blair government's neo-Thatcherite policies in health and education. Even more, it voiced a collective instinct that an era in world history, the short post-cold war era in which US power seemed invincible, is over.

Many analysts still forecast a swift, decisive war; but it is hard to see how that will rescue Blair if it is followed by a rapid slide into chaos. The geopolitical fissures that have been opened up by America's march to war yawn ever wider. Blair has said that history will judge him. It may do so sooner than he thinks.

March 10, 2003

17

WASHINGTON'S NEW JACOBINS

Around two hundred years ago, the great French reactionary thinker Joseph de Maistre wrote of 'the profound imbecility of those poor men who imagine that nations can be constituted with ink'. De Maistre, one of the fiercest critics of the Enlightenment, was targeting the radical *philosophes*, who believed that liberal republics could be established throughout the world. Against this sunny view, de Maistre insisted that nations are made from human suffering, as different cultures and traditions clash in unending historical conflict.

In de Maistre's day, it was the French Jacobins who believed that democracy could be spread throughout the world by fiat; today it is American neo-conservatives. There are many differences between the two, some of them profound: the sense of mission that animates the Bush administration owes as much to Christian fundamentalism as it does to Enlightenment universalism. Yet American neo-conservatives are at one with the French Jacobins on the most essential, and most dangerously misguided, point. Both are convinced that democratic government can be made universal, and in pretty short order.

To be sure, they also know that more than ink is required to realize this noble ideal. The Jacobins understood very well that blood would also have to be spilt. Equally, the neo-conservative intellectuals who are calling the shots at the White House accept that terror will be necessary; but, like their Jacobin predecessors, they believe it will be just and merciful, a brief pang before the advent of a new world. A think-tank warrior such as Richard Perle may think of himself as a realist, but the cold frenzy with which he urges war reminds one more of Robespierre than Metternich. Like their Jacobin predecessors, Perle and his neo-conservative confreres believe they can rewrite history and bring humanity to unprecedented freedom and harmony.

We have seen the awful consequences in Iraq: the people of that unhappy country, much as they hate Saddam Hussein, have not embraced the American invaders in quite the way that Washington hoped. And the rest of us are compelled to face an awful truth: that though we, too, wish for the sudden collapse of Saddam's regime, a swift and decisive American victory, even if it comes about, can only embolden the Bush administration in its revolutionary new policies. Flushed with victory, the neo-conservatives would be ready to embark on a project of reconfiguring global politics as far-reaching as any attempted in the twentieth century, exporting US-style democracy to the Middle East and thereby guaranteeing America's global hegemony.

The hawks now fully in charge of Washington policy spurn multinational institutions and scorn the traditional arts of diplomacy. They have turned their backs on the policies of deterrence and containment that preserved the world from disaster in the cold war. Instead, applying the new doctrine of preventive war, they are determined to eradicate threats to

American power wherever they perceive them; but their objectives go far beyond simply defending the US from attack. They aim to entrench American global hegemony against any potential challenge. In their view, this demands more than disabling 'rogue states' (such as Saddam's Iraq) and putting friendly regimes in place. It requires reshaping post-war Iraq and much of the rest of the Middle East in an American image. After Iraq, Iran and Syria are in line for regime change. The entire region is to be reshaped to reflect American values.

This fantastical scheme will be tested to destruction in post-war Iraq. Current US pronouncements on rebuilding the country change from one day to the next and need not be taken too seriously, but it is clear that the Bush administration means to govern Iraq itself, with the UK serving, as ever, as its obedient junior partner, and the UN and the EU playing only a peripheral role. With transnational institutions marginalized, the Americans will face a major problem in legitimating their occupation of Iraq in the Arab world and, for that matter, the world as a whole.

Perhaps with this in mind, they talk of holding democratic elections in the country within a year. They say they want Iraq to be a self-governing nation; but Iraq is not and has never been a nation state. Under Saddam, it has evolved into an extremely repressive regime in which power and privilege are concentrated in a single clan and its hangers-on; but it remains a multinational state, in some ways not unlike the former Yugoslavia. 'The Iraqi people' does not exist. The country comprises several distinct ethnic and religious groupings, which have been at one another's throats for many years. Along with some elements in the fractious Iraqi opposition, the Americans talk of a federal Iraq in which these groups will live peacefully together. But history shows that such constructions are extremely fragile. Democracy, above all the federal variety, requires trust, but trust is a commodity in desperately short supply in communities divided by historical memories of savage conflict.

As events in the Balkans have shown, when an authoritarian multinational state collapses, the result is not federalism. It is war and ethnic cleansing. The threat that Turkish forces will move into zones claimed by the Kurds is just the first sign of the bloody fragmentation that may lie in store for Iraq. To think that democracy can be established under such conditions is not just far-fetched, it is imbecilic.

From one angle, then, the Bush administration's project in Iraq is an exercise in the most radical utopianism. From another, it is pure geopolitics. Public statements show that the hawks in the White House and among the Pentagon's civilian leadership see the war as part of a grand strategy to shore up American hegemony, not just in the Middle East but throughout the world. This is where Iraq's oil comes in: not so much as a secure source of supply for America's profligate energy users, but as a lever against potential challenges to US supremacy. Remember the first Gulf war. That war was fought – rightly, as I still think – to stop Saddam gaining control of the oil supplies of Kuwait and Saudi Arabia, and so acquiring a stranglehold over the global economy. The second Gulf war is being fought to enable the US – and only the US – to seize the same prize. Controlling Iraq's oil will not only allow the US to loosen its ties with Saudi Arabia and break the power of OPEC. It will give the US a powerful weapon against states that it regards as strategic rivals; above all, China. Over the next decade or so, as industrialization gathers speed, China will become heavily dependent on oil supplies from the Gulf. So, still, will much of the rest of the world. If the Americans succeed in Iraq, they will have achieved what Saddam sought in vain a dozen years ago, an unchallengeable hold over the global economy.

The mismatch between the Bush administration's schemes for post-war Iraq and its geopolitical goals is clear enough. What is less clear is how this disconnection will be resolved. There is a widespread view in Europe, Asia and parts of the Middle East that, when the US discovers how difficult it is to govern post-war Iraq, it will do what it always does in such circumstances: pack up and leave others to police the ruins.

Ruling post-war Iraq will be even more demanding than ruling Afghanistan. It will involve more than rebuilding its infrastructure, a vast enterprise that the US, with its ballooning budget deficits and sagging economy, cannot sustain. It requires a willingness to accept casualties.

Will American voters be ready to pay, in higher taxes and a steady flow of body bags, the price of the Bush administration's grand strategy? If not, it is hard to see how the US can remain in Iraq for the long haul. Yet its retreat would amount to a devastating defeat, even in the aftermath of an overwhelming military victory. American power would be damaged beyond repair.

America's war in Iraq is the brainchild of neo-conservative intellectuals who despise the traditional diplomacy of the State Department and the seasoned caution of the professional soldiers at the Pentagon. Like the Jacobins in the late eighteenth century and Lenin's Bolsheviks in the early twentieth, the

American neo-conservatives who are now calling the shots at the White House are revolutionary intellectuals with a very hazy view of the world in which most of humanity actually lives.

They do not grasp the depth and intensity of the hatred with which American power is viewed in the Middle East. They have closed their ears to the derision with which America is discussed in much of Europe and Asia, in sharp contrast to the wide admiration it enjoyed in the wake of 11 September. They have shut out of their minds awkward questions about how counter-terrorist strategies can be effective when some of the countries that know most about the threat, notably France, may in future be less ready to co-operate with the US. They appear unaware of the mounting risks of trade war that go with the threat of American economic sanctions against European countries such as France and Germany. With all their talk of weapons of mass destruction, they seem oblivious to the accelerating proliferation produced by their own rejection of arms control agreements. They are animated by the faith that American firepower can protect America from attack; but America's superiority in high-tech weaponry cannot protect it against the sort of asymmetric warfare practised by Osama Bin Laden.

This is an alarming state of affairs, but it is not surprising. It is a natural result of the bizarre world-view of the neo-conservatives who have taken America into Iraq. An exotic mix of Dr Strangelove and Dr Billy Graham, they believe that once the war is won they can convert the Middle East to US-style democracy. As Joseph de Maistre knew, such attempts to rewrite history always end in tears. The dark forebodings of that sage of old Europe may have missed the gains in human well-being that were being achieved even as he lived; but they were borne out by the murderous history of the twentieth century. It looks like they will be vindicated again.

March 31, 2003

18

THE MIRAGE OF AMERICAN EMPIRE

When Donald Rumsfeld declared that peace could be achieved only by unconditional surrender he revealed a crucial flaw in the Bush administration's thinking about the war in Iraq. With the destruction of Saddam Hussein's regime, there is no authority left in the country with the power to enforce surrender. A modern western police state has been replaced by pre-modern anarchy. Like other failed states such as Afghanistan, post-war Iraq will be the site of unconventional warfare for generations to come.

The reality is that the war has not ended but instead entered a new phase. Iraq's would-be liberators are now the targets of Chechen-style guerrilla resistance from sections of Iraq's diverse and fractious population. At the same time, in the absence of any internationally legitimate alternative, the occupying forces will be expected to keep the peace, a forbiddingly difficult task that is made almost impossible by the lack of the necessary manpower. With Iraq a stateless zone, only British and American forces can ensure a semblance of order; but they have been equipped for a short war and not for the long haul of neo-colonial rule that is now the only way of keeping anarchy at bay.

Though it was entirely predictable, the chaos of post-war Iraq figured nowhere in the plans of the ideologues who engineered the war. The neo-cons in the civilian leadership of the Pentagon saw the war as a conflict between states: one of them the world's military mega-power, the other a ramshackle tyranny whose resources had been depleted by twelve years of sanctions and bombing. Self-evidently, there could be only one outcome in such a conflict. But the neo-cons were wildly optimistic about the condition of post-war Iraq. Providing the rudiments of government in such chaos poses almost insoluble difficulties.

It is not only that the occupying forces have no clear mandate in international law and are viewed throughout the Arab world as invaders, but also that the strategic objectives and rules of engagement of the US and British forces are vague or incoherent. Why are they there? Is it to find and dismantle weapons of mass destruction, as Tony Blair kept on telling us right up to the outbreak of war? Is it to replace an unpleasant tyranny by some sort of democracy, as he and President Bush are telling us today? Or is the invasion and occupation of Iraq simply the first in a series of regime changes designed to remake the world in an American image, as several neo-con ideologues with powerful friends in the Bush administration have repeatedly asserted?

These are not just theoretical questions. How they are answered determines how British and US forces treat Iraq's civilian population. The US forces insist that they want to liberate Iraq. Yet the Pentagon's doctrine of 'force protection', which makes saving American lives the paramount consideration in any military operation, requires them to treat all Iraqis as potential enemies. Applying this doctrine, American forces are behaving in Iraq as they did in the Balkans: engaging with ordinary people as little as possible, and then only under the cover of maximum force. The policy can only bolster the perception of the Americans as aggressors.

The British forces are responding far more subtly and effectively. Long experience has taught them that maintaining any kind of order in a semi-anarchic environment such as post-war Iraq demands close and sensitive engagement with the local people. But it is not the British who call the shots. If, as seems likely, the American forces come under persistent and increasing attack from people dressed in civilian clothes, they will inevitably respond by trying to insulate themselves from the population as a whole.

The failure to anticipate the scale and depth of the breakdown of civil order in post-war Iraq was of a piece with the childish unrealism of neo-conservative thinking. In much of Europe, the neo-con intellectuals who engineered the war in Iraq are seen as Machiavellians whose evil machinations portend an era of unrestrained American hegemony. The truth is more bizarre, and perhaps more alarming. The true believers at the Pentagon and the White House are not conservatives in any sense that is familiar in Europe. They are callow utopians with scant understanding of the intractable problems of the world they are so eager to remake. The plan of the US deputy secretary of defence, Paul Wolfowitz, to install American-style democracy throughout the Middle East is not realistic. It is a messianic fantasy, whose principal enduring result will be to weaken America's remaining allies in the region, such as Jordan and Egypt.

Far from entrenching US hegemony, the effect of neo-con policies is to undermine it. The media spectacle of American firepower laying waste to sections of Baghdad has not diminished the loathing in which the US is held throughout the Arab world. Instead the overpowering superiority of the US in high-tech warfare is increasing the appeal of terrorism. There is a dark irony in the rise of suicide bombing in Iraq. Like the Palestinian territories, Iraq has been one of the most secular societies in the Middle East. Now, as a by-product of a war waged with the avowed aim of promoting 'western liberal values', a fundamentalist culture of martyrdom is taking hold. How order can be maintained in the country under these conditions is anyone's guess, but – as was anticipated in assessments made by the Pentagon and by the British military many months ago, only to be rejected by Donald Rumsfeld – it is likely to require hundreds of thousands of troops stationed there indefinitely.

Here we have the nub of the dilemma. The neo-cons have embarked on a grandiose project of regime change throughout the Middle East. In any realistic assessment, such a venture would demand a decades-long American military presence and a similar commitment to nation-building – in other words, the establishment of something akin to an American imperium in the region. Plainly, however, the Bush administration has no interest in nation-building, and nothing but contempt for peacekeeping. As Condoleezza Rice remarked only the other day, the American forces are not in Iraq to make sure children get safely to school.

In fact, if America's invasion of Iraq is indeed the first move in establishing some sort of neo-imperial governance in the Middle East, this is exactly the kind of duty that US forces will have to learn to discharge. Yet it is hard to think of any major power so ill-equipped to sustain the burdens of empire. Culturally, the US has little tolerance for a steady flow of body bags. Economically, its capacity to support an imperial role is dubious. If Americans want empire at all, it is on the cheap: without the casualties or the expense.

Given the scale of the quandaries facing the Americans in Iraq, it may seem unthinkable that there are some in the Bush administration who talk about widening the war. Many people in Britain tend to dismiss these voices, arguing that as a pragmatic politician Bush will want to show he is concerned with the health of the US economy and other domestic issues.

I am not so sure. The war has distracted public attention from the US economy's difficulties. It is just possible that it can continue to do so until the presidential election next autumn. An expansion of the war would be consistent with the doctrine of pre-empting threats to American national security, as announced by Bush in Congress in September 2002. Indeed, a shift to a wider war may already be under way. Over the past week or so, al-Qaeda has ceased to be central in White House briefings on the 'war against terror'. Hamas and Hezbollah are the new targets. In the Middle East this is being read as a clear indication that the policy of regime change will soon be extended to Syria and Iran.

Such a widening of the war would be catastrophically destabilizing, and not only for the countries of the Middle East. It would solidify the 'anti-American axis', with China and perhaps India lining up behind France, Germany and Russia. In Britain, this near-complete isolation of the US from the rest of the international community would mean greatly increased political risks for Blair. With the fall of Baghdad, the threat to the Prime Minister seemed to vanish, but if Britain were to follow the US into a wider Middle Eastern war it would return with a vengeance.

Even as things stand, Blair's position is not as safe as it looks. He has again staked his future on a pledge on which he cannot deliver. The 'road map' to self-determination for the Palestinians promised by Bush is extremely unlikely ever to amount to anything of substance. Given the domestic political risks, it is hard to see what incentive Bush has to carry it through, aside from repaying Blair's loyalty. Cordially detested as he is by some of Bush's closest advisers, Blair may be unwise to rely on the president's gratitude.

Whether or not the war spreads beyond Iraq, it has already altered Britain's place in the world. In the view of some American right-wing commentators, Blair's unblinking support of US policy has had the effect of detaching Britain from the rest of Europe. Britain's future, they argue, lies in the 'Anglosphere', an English-speaking union centred on the US. Excluding, as it does, Canada and New Zealand, which have had the good sense to opt out of the Bush administration's military adventures, the Anglosphere is a fatuous notion. Still, the right-wing commentators have a point. Blair's decision to join Bush in prosecuting an unnecessary, quite possibly illegal and certainly criminally stupid war has alienated him deeply and very likely irreversibly from the core countries of Continental Europe. Anyone who thinks that Britain can be 'at the heart of Europe' while Blair is Prime Minister has failed to grasp this shift in European attitudes. In present circumstances, any attempt by Blair to join the euro might even be derailed by a veto.

So is Britain bound to drift ever further from the rest of Europe? On the contrary, the long-term impact of war in Iraq could well work the other way. Blair has entangled Britain in a dangerous conflict that has no clear end point. It is a war that serves no British national interest. It is the result of applying a neo-conservative world-view in which Blair sincerely believes, but which is detested by the overwhelming majority in his party and viewed with suspicion by most people in the country. Despite the Prime Minister's current popularity, these are circumstances that do not augur well for him. If Blair finds his survival once again in question as a result of his support for this war, his difficulties will send a powerful message to the British political class. In its attitudes to war and peace, Britain is a European country. It has no taste for global crusades. When that message sinks in, Britain will begin its drift away from America and into Europe.

April 21, 2003

19

IRAQ AND THE ILLUSIONS OF GLOBAL GOVERNANCE

Many who opposed the war in Iraq now demand that the country be placed under international administration. They believe the UN can give the country what it did not have under Saddam Hussein and still lacks today: a legitimate government. Turning to the UN expresses the liberal faith that the world is evolving towards a form of global governance. It also accords with fashionable ideas of globalization according to which the power of sovereign states is steadily waning.

Yet the UN would not be able to pacify and rebuild Iraq, and it should keep a safe distance from the ugly guerrilla war that is brewing there. The last thing the world needs is another misguided and ineffectual exercise in liberal imperialism. The lesson of the disastrous adventure in Iraq is just the opposite: the old-fashioned principle of state sovereignty must be reaffirmed as the basis of peaceful coexistence in a pluralistic world.

Rather than turning to the UN, we should be looking to democratic politics in the US and Britain. The blowback of war in Iraq will mount over the coming months. Almost certainly, casualties among the invaders will increase significantly. At the same time, the deception that accompanied the war

from its inception will come home to roost. The Bush administration is likely to be weakened and Tony Blair's position may
become untenable.

It is easy to be carried away by the ongoing saga of the
'dodgy dossier' and the role of the BBC, and impossible not to
be moved by the death of David Kelly. However, by focusing
on these sordid and tragic events, we risk missing the bigger
picture. The Iraq war could not have been sold to the public
without extensive disinformation. In the US, it was sold by
propagating the belief that Saddam was somehow involved
with al-Qaeda in the terrorist attacks of 11 September 2001.
There was never a jot of evidence for this link. Al-Qaeda's
brand of theocratic anarchism is light years away from
Saddam's militant secularism, and captured al-Qaeda opera-
tives have testified that Osama Bin Laden rejected any
co-operation with the Iraqi regime. But the hawks in the Bush
administration did not see the absence of any solid information connecting al-Qaeda with Saddam as a reason for
thinking that none existed. It was viewed as a defect in the
available intelligence. As Greg Thielmann, a former official at
the US State Department, recently observed, the hawks in the
administration had a 'faith-based' approach to intelligence.
Their attitude was: 'We know the answers. Give us the intelligence to support those answers.'

In Britain, the war was sold by invoking the threat posed by
Saddam's supposed weapons of mass destruction. But the
architects of the war in Washington have always seen the
WMD issue as peripheral, and now dismiss it as irrelevant. In
an interview with *Vanity Fair*, Paul Wolfowitz, the US deputy
defence secretary, reported that he had settled on the WMD
issue as the main justification for the war 'for bureaucratic

reasons', given that it was the one reason everyone could agree on. Speaking recently to reporters aboard an air force jet returning to Washington after a tour of Iraq, Wolfowitz went further, describing WMDs as a 'historical issue' with which he was not concerned.

Blair may have persuaded himself that the Bush administration's claims about Iraq's weapons were well founded, and it is not inconceivable that they contained some truth. But they were never more than a pretext for war; neither Britain nor the US was ever at risk from Saddam. As Wolfowitz acknowledged in the *Vanity Fair* interview, the administration's geopolitical objectives had to do with facilitating America's withdrawal from Saudi Arabia. This required toppling Saddam and securing US control of Iraqi oil. More broadly, for many of those who engineered the war, it was a means of fomenting a 'democratic revolution' throughout the Middle East, as a result of which the balance of power in the region would shift towards the US and its allies.

The true strategic goals of the war in Iraq are hardly secret. Yet they were not the objectives cited by Bush and Blair when they defended the decision to attack Iraq. This is the crucial fact about the war, and the reason it is sure to rebound badly on Bush and even more so on Blair. It was fought for reasons that were never stated. As a result, it has never had democratic legitimacy.

If Bush and Blair deceived the public about the reasons for going to war, they deceived themselves about its impact on Iraq. There was never the remotest possibility that the invading forces would be accepted as liberators. The US and Britain were instrumental in enforcing a brutal blockade on the country. The policy may have been justified by the lack of any better alternative, but Iraqis saw it as punishing them for the sins of their ruler. In any case, why should Iraqis welcome the invasion and occupation of their country? It is a question that will become more, not less, urgent once Saddam is killed or in American hands. The Americans are staking everything on their strategy of decapitation: once the Ba'athist state has been beheaded, they believe, resistance will scatter and fade away. They overlook the possibility that attacks on the occupying forces are mostly the work of Islamists, not remnants of the Ba'athist regime. If this is so, Saddam's death or capture will not stem these attacks. On the contrary, by removing one big reason for tolerating the US presence, it is likely to draw more of the population into armed resistance.

The war in Iraq has not ended but merely moved into a new phase. A brief and decisive encounter of armies is being followed by something more like the intractable, unconventional warfare practised by al-Qaeda. The groups that are attacking the occupying forces in Iraq are very unlikely to be acting at the behest of any directing authority. If they are co-ordinated at all, it is by their reactions to the news media. Following the worldwide security crackdown after 11 September 2001, al-Qaeda seems to have renewed itself as a loose network of affinity groups united principally by a common way of thinking. Islamist resistance in Iraq may be developing in a similar way, in which case the country is in for a long period of guerrilla war.

The deteriorating situation in Iraq is a predictable result of a war that was ill-conceived from the start. To turn to the UN for salvation is just another exercise in wishful thinking. Set aside the fact that to seek help from that quarter, the US would have to swallow its pride. The Bush administration may already be sufficiently intimidated by the quandary it has got itself into for such a humbling reversal of attitudes to be imaginable. The difficulty comes more from the appalling task the UN would have to take on in Iraq. As is clear from Afghanistan, policing a collapsed state is a dangerous and potentially interminable business. In the case of Iraq, the risk is that UN forces would be seen as proxies for the US army of occupation. It is hard to imagine a more daunting set of circumstances for peacekeepers. Why should the French, the Russians or the rest of the international community that opposed the war take on the thankless task of cleaning up the mess the Americans have made? Throughout the Middle East, it is not UN involvement that is being demanded, but American withdrawal.

The idea that the UN can rectify the mistakes of a great power is clearly an illusion, but it is of a piece with a larger illusion about the possibilities of global governance. Ever since the end of the cold war, opinion-formers have been infatuated with the idea that power is ebbing away from sovereign states. Globalization is forcing a continuous transfer of the functions of governance to transnational institutions, they tell us, and the world of sovereign states belongs in the past. Like many other fashionable delusions, this belief is based on extrapolating from a short and untypical period in history – the dozen years between the fall of the Berlin Wall and the terrorist attacks on 11 September 2001 – into the indefinite future. During that time, many academics and politicians came to believe that we are moving into a post-Westphalian world. Misreading the relative peace of that unquiet interregnum for a stable condition, and viewing history as a progressive movement towards a universal civilization, they look forward to a time when the anarchy of sovereign states has given way to a form of global governance.

There are many blind spots in this credulous vision, not least its view of the UN as an embryonic version of world government. In reality, like the League of Nations, the UN is a forum created and sustained by sovereign states and liable to be abandoned by them when it stands in the way of the pursuit of their interests. Far from moving into a post-Westphalian world, we have entered one in which sovereign states are reclaiming their powers. This is most obviously true of the most powerful among them. The US has signed off from a number of treaties. It is adamantly opposed to its citizens becoming subject to the jurisdiction of the International Criminal Court. It cannot be long before it thumbs its nose at the World Trade Organization. What we are witnessing here are not the teething troubles of a post-Westphalian world. They are the beginnings of a new era of state sovereignty.

On the left, the revival of the sovereign state will be seen as an unmitigated disaster. Among bien-pensant economists, besotted with the vision of a worldwide free market, it will be greeted with shock and horror. No one should doubt that this is a development fraught with dangers. But it brings with it one crucial benefit: political decisions are returned to a level at which they can be subject to democratic accountability.

The power of transnational institutions is not subject to any kind of democratic control. In practice, it is almost always used to further the interests of the strongest states. Throughout the 1990s, the International Monetary Fund and the World Bank were little more than instruments whereby the US imposed a self-serving economic orthodoxy on weak and developing states. Now that its economy is in serious trouble, the US has lost interest in the niceties of free trade and the balanced budget. It will certainly not allow itself to be dictated to by any of the transnational organizations it supported so vociferously in the recent past.

Conventional wisdom will view the revival of state sovereignty as a recipe for a war of all against all, but it is nothing so apocalyptic. It is simply a return to a more diverse international environment of a kind that was accepted as normal in the past. It was only with the rise of secular religions such as communism and neo-liberalism in the twentieth century that it came to be widely believed that all human beings should live under the same institutions.

At the start of the twenty-first century, our most urgent need is not to revisit these discredited utopias. It is to devise means whereby regimes that will always be different can achieve some kind of modus vivendi. The UN will have a pivotal role in this task, but it will be the modest one of framing minimal terms of peaceful coexistence among sovereign states.

For Blair, the war in Iraq is a test case of a new world based on curbing state sovereignty (always excepting that of the US). He has made it clear that Iraq is not a one-off affair, but the application of a new doctrine of international relations. 'Rogue states' are to be destroyed, and a version of liberal democracy promoted universally. It is a vision that clearly appeals to Blair's messianic tendencies, but it leaves out a crucial fact. The states that are engaged in fighting this holy war for democracy are themselves democracies.

However imperfect they may be, the US and Britain remain countries whose leaders can be peacefully removed by their citizens. President Bush is likely to be weakened as the casualties mount in a war that many Americans have never supported. Even so, still riding high on the moral authority conferred on him by the 11 September 2001 attacks, Bush may be proof against the most damaging fallout from the war. Blair is considerably more vulnerable. When he took Britain into this war, his supporters claimed he would emerge from it strengthened. As could be foreseen, it has damaged him irreparably.

A fatal air of unreality hangs over Blair's entire programme. His campaign to reform public services is a laughing stock. The idea that he can persuade voters of the need to enter the single currency is even more ludicrous. Granted a run of luck, Blair may struggle on for a while, but his government will be a lame duck; one more shock and he will be gone. The new world order is on a collision course with political reality. The war in Iraq was never going to bring freedom to that unhappy country, but it may yet show that democracy is alive in Britain.

August 4, 2003

PART 3

POLITICS WITHOUT ILLUSIONS

20

THE DARK SIDE OF MODERNITY:
EUROPE'S NEW FAR RIGHT

In the lexicon of contemporary cant, modernization signifies everything that is worth striving for. Who wants to be backward, or worse still, reactionary? Being modern, we think, is good; not being modern is bad. And progressive thinkers take for granted that being modern means accepting liberal values. Yet many of the most repressive regimes in recent history have been uncompromisingly modern. Even the Nazis, who mobilized Europe's deeply rooted traditions of racism and anti-Semitism, did so in the service of a modern revolutionary project. It has become an article of faith that the growth of the global economy goes hand in hand with the spread of liberal values. Yet across Europe, parties that reject liberal values are entering deeply into the political mainstream. Conventional wisdom on the centre left explains this development by the failure of mainstream parties to defend multicultural ideals and the economic advantages of immigration. The truth is less reassuring. Today, as in much of the twentieth century, it is the enemies of liberal societies who best understand their fragility.

Among the parties of the far right across the Channel, an

ambitious new project of modernization is under way. In Britain, modernization means becoming a centrist party, the hugely successful strategy adopted by Labour on its way back to power. In Continental Europe, it is the strategy through which the far right is breaking the hold of the centre on power. Europe's far-right parties encompass a variety of tendencies. What they have in common is that they use the social dislocation produced by the global free market, now the chief icon of modernization, as fuel for a new politics of identity. Far better than its fumbling centre parties, Europe's far right knows that globalization has losers, even in the richest countries. By linking the fears of these people with high levels of immigration, the far right is mounting a powerful challenge to the centrist consensus that has ruled most of Continental Europe since the end of the cold war. At the same time, the advance of the far right confounds the faith which underpins progressive thinking everywhere; that democracy and prosperity ensure a liberal, cosmopolitan future.

There are continuities between pre-war fascist and Nazi movements and the European far right today, but what we are seeing is not simply a replay of the events of the 1930s. Then, secular ideologies were at odds in much of the world, and mass political parties struggled for control of powerful states. Now, secular ideology is in retreat and there are no mass political parties. When large numbers of people are mobilized today, it is in fundamentalist movements or in single-issue groups such as Greenpeace, or in amorphous networks such as the anti-capitalist activists. Europe contains no totalitarian states of the kind that were common between the wars. Corrupt and semi-authoritarian as it may be in some of the post-communist countries, democratic governance is entrenched throughout Europe.

Nor is Europe, outside Russia and the Balkans, at any rate, scarred by economic crisis. Not only in Germany, but in much of Continental Europe, the far right came to power between the wars on the back of hyperinflation and mass unemployment. Today's far right has made some of its most striking gains in some of the most prosperous countries. By no stretch of the imagination can Austria be said to be on the brink of economic crisis: it has one of the lowest rates of unemployment in Europe, along with one of the most highly developed welfare states. Yet it was in Austria that Jorg Haider's Freedom Party overturned a 30-year centrist consensus and became a partner in the national government. Again, the rise of Pim Fortuyn cannot be explained by unemployment, which is even lower in the Netherlands than in Austria.

To think of the far right as merely atavistic is to underestimate it. Whereas between the wars Europe's far right gained strength from poverty and economic crisis, today it thrives on the insecurities of the affluent. Using democracy rather than seeking to overturn it, the far right is redrawing the map of European politics by exploiting the fears of voters in rich countries.

In its economic philosophy, it is the acme of modernity. Most of Europe's far-right parties have abandoned the protectionist programme of the inter-war years. Except in France, where Jean-Marie Le Pen continues the murky traditions of Vichy, the far right is libertarian in its economic outlook. In Austria, Switzerland and northern Italy, it promotes a high-tech economy linked with the world by free trade but insulated from the legions of the poor by a ban on immigration. If this is fascism, it is the fascism of laptops, not jackboots. Like the fascist parties of the past, the far right accepts the economic orthodoxies of its time. Today, those are the orthodoxies of the free market.

Along with the centre parties, the far right has embraced globalization. Unlike the centre parties, however, it understands that the global market has casualties. It may be true that global free trade sometimes benefits poor people in poor countries (though the evidence for this is not overwhelming), but, as its less doctrinaire enthusiasts are ready to admit, it does nothing for unskilled manual workers in rich countries. Equally – and this may prove to be more important politically – it has few benefits for office workers and middle managers whose functions can be downloaded to parts of the world where labour is cheaper. Even where they do not now suffer from high levels of unemployment, those manual workers and white-collar employees whose tasks can be automated tend to have incomes that fall behind the rest of society. For these groups, globalization means inexorable decline.

The strategic coup of the far right has been to blame immigrants, themselves often victims of globalization in poor parts of the world, for the casualties of globalization in Europe. It is a success made possible by deep-seated European traditions of xenophobia and racism. Here there are some ominous echoes of the worst parts of Europe's history. Except in the Netherlands, anti-Semitism remains at the core of the far right. Le Pen's National Front stands firmly in a tradition that goes back to Charles Maurras's Action Française, a radical nationalist-monarchist organization founded in 1899 and embodying the political anti-Semitism of the Third Republic, which culminated in the Dreyfus case. In recent years, the far right's anti-Semitism has become more open and brazen. A senior member of the Vlaams Blok in Belgium has cast doubt on the reality of the Holocaust and questioned the authenticity of the diaries of Anne Frank. By doing so, he revealed the underlying agenda of the far right across nearly all of Europe. Today, as in the past, the dark side of Europe's communitarian traditions and prized social cohesion is the exclusion of minorities and foreigners. The centre parties find it impossible to admit the strength and depth of Europe's fear and hatred of outsiders. The far right has no such inhibitions.

In its use of European racism, the far right today resembles its counterpart between the wars. But there are important differences. Hard-core radical fascists were often contemptuous of nationalism. In Arthur Koestler's wartime novel, *Arrival and Departure*, he has a philosophizing Nazi diplomat – a type which actually existed in Europe at that time – assert that Nazism is more internationalist than the French revolution or communism, a revolutionary project that will wipe out Europe's 'anachronistic national sovereignties'. In the Nazis' New Order, Jews will be exterminated, along with gypsies, and small nations relocated where they can be most useful to the pan-European economy:

'Close your eyes. Imagine Europe up to the Urals as an empty space on the map. There are only fields of energy . . . Wipe out those ridiculous winding boundaries, the Chinese walls which cuts across our fields of energy; scrap or transfer industries that were heedlessly built in the wrong places; liquidate the surplus population in areas where they are not required; shift the population of certain districts, if necessary of entire nations, to the spaces where they are wanted, and to the type of production for which they are most racially fitted.'

Although it lingered on in Oswald Mosley's post-war slogan 'Europe: a nation', this anti-nationalist strand in far-right thinking largely died out after 1945. Today, all of Europe's far-right parties are markedly hostile to European institutions. But it is worth remembering the Nazi intelligentsia's contempt for nationalism because it is of a piece with their overall modernism. In Germany and Italy, the far right recruited supporters from avant-garde cultural movements such as expressionism and futurism. Again, the Nazis embraced modern science: Adolf Hitler was a passionate partisan of technology as an instrument of human power, including the power to commit genocide on an unprecedented scale. As Koestler's Nazi diplomat declares: 'We have embarked on something gigantic beyond imagination. There are no more impossibilities for man now. For the first time we are attacking the biological structure of the species. We have started to breed a new species of Homo sapiens. We are weeding out its streaks of bad heredity. We have practically finished the task of exterminating or sterilizing the gypsies in Europe; the liquidation of the Jews will be completed in a year or two . . . We are the first to make use of the hypodermic syringe, the lancet and the sterilizing apparatus in our revolution.'

Attitudes of this kind were not confined to Nazis. George Bernard Shaw advocated mass extermination as a humane alternative to imprisonment, lauded Stalinist Russia at a time when millions were dying of starvation and viewed Hitler's Germany as a progressive regime. H G Wells flirted with similar views. For these thinkers of the left, as for the Nazis themselves, Nazism was the opposite of a reactionary movement. It was an embodiment of one of the core beliefs of the modern period: the faith that progress demands the use of science and technology to transform the human condition, without regard to the moralities of the past. If the Second World War had ended differently and the Nazis had prevailed in Europe, who is to say that the New Order they would have imposed would not have been modern?

The far right was a radical modernist movement in the 1930s, and so it is today. Now, as in the past, it appeals to voters for more traditional right-wing parties, but its widening support includes the much larger ranks of the politically disaffected. Nowhere is this clearer than in the Netherlands, where Pim Fortuyn showed the strategy of the far right at its most subtle. An ex-Marxist and former academic, Fortuyn was neo-Thatcherite on the economy and the environment, harping on the evils of regulation and the burdens of taxation. Yet, unlike Thatcherites in Britain, he favoured a highly liberal regime on sex, euthanasia and drug use. Again, he took a firm pro-Israel line on conflict in the Middle East and does not seem to have been anti-Semitic. But he undoubtedly played the race card, particularly against Muslims, and he did so, at least by his own account, because he believed that further Muslim immigration would threaten Dutch freedoms of lifestyle: he challenged the belief that liberal societies should assimilate immigrants whose values are anti-liberal. In effect, he advocated a policy of liberal cultural protectionism. He failed to explain how such a policy could be implemented in places where, as in the Netherlands and throughout Europe, multiculturalism is an irreversible reality. Partly for this reason, it seems unlikely that his party will be effective in government. Even so, Fortuyn's legacy is the destruction of the Dutch liberal consensus.

*

Across Europe, the centre is losing its hold. Far-right parties are already in national government in Austria, Italy, Denmark and the Netherlands. Yet Europe's political elites remain stubbornly resistant to the message this sends. In part, no doubt, it is simply the complacency of power, even if that power is fading fast. But it is also an intellectual default. Since the end of the cold war, all mainstream parties have accepted the same ideology, according to which economic modernization and liberal values advance in tandem. Leave aside the belief that the free market is the only path to economic modernity. Even if this were not a historical myth, the notion that a modernized economy is bound somehow to engender a liberal society would still be a fantasy. Market reform has advanced in China and, more recently, in Russia without making any concessions to liberal ideas about human rights. There is no reason why the same should not happen in other parts of the world. The link between liberal values and economic growth is a historical accident, not a universal law.

To be sure, bien-pensant economists will tell you that, over time, prosperity must lead to a demand for personal freedom; but there is little evidence for this comfortable belief. In much of Continental Europe, where the far right makes headway against a background of low unemployment and general prosperity, it is plainly mistaken. That does not mean it will be abandoned. The belief that free markets and liberal values go together is not a result of empirical inquiry. It is a confession of faith: the Enlightenment faith that, with the growth of knowledge and wealth, human beings will shed their various, divisive identities to become members of a universal civilization. Once the prerogative of Marxists, this fanciful rationalistic creed is now the intellectual basis of market reform throughout the world.

It lies behind the argument, now as commonplace as the clamour for privatization a decade or so ago, that demographic factors make further immigration an economic necessity. It may be true that an ageing Europe could benefit from a steady flow of immigrants— though so long as some European countries have more than 10 per cent of their workforces unemployed, the argument is hardly conclusive. But even if its economic benefits are great, large-scale immigration carries high political risks. In the late nineteenth century, few borders mattered, and labour had virtually as much freedom of movement as capital. This is a phase of globalization that many economists, and not a few on the left, view with something approaching nostalgia; but it was also a period in which democracy was limited, trade unions weak and the welfare state non-existent. By contrast, in Europe today, where welfare states and trade unions are strong, persuading voters to accept open borders must be a forbiddingly difficult task.

It is true that a democratic consensus in favour of liberal immigration policies exists in the United States. But America's openness to immigrants testifies to its success in forging a national identity that transcends ethnic origins, an achievement that cannot be replicated across Europe. European institutions cannot replace national identities, but they are widely perceived as eroding them. Weakened national cultures do not cope well with the difficulties of assimilating newcomers; they are breeding grounds for a vicious populist politics that seeks to buttress identity through ethnic exclusion. Riddled with ancient bigotries, uncertain of its future and its place in the world, Europe has contrived to weaken national identities at a time when the legitimacy of its institutions has never been more widely questioned. It is a dangerous place to launch an experiment in liberal utopianism.

The far right understands the frailty of liberal societies; the centre parties do not. Sustained by a combination of hubris, fashionable doctrine and a comforting ignorance of history, Europe's political elites seem determined to deny the mounting risks. As a result, in not much more than a few years, they are likely to find themselves partners in power with the far right across much of the continent. Once again, Europe looks set to give birth to a version of modernity that encompasses its darkest traditions.

June 24, 2002

21

FOR EUROPE'S SAKE, BRITAIN MUST STAY OUT

A referendum on the euro is unlikely before the next election, mainly because Tony Blair, having survived a real risk to his premiership over the Iraq war, will not want to push his luck too far. But if the Prime Minister does gamble his future again, true Europeans must hope that he fails.

This is one of the paradoxes of the European debate in Britain. Among those who oppose British integration into the EU, few understand that the most likely effect of Britain remaining semi-detached will be to speed the evolution of something resembling a European state. Equally, those who fervently yearn for Britain to enter more closely into European institutions rarely grasp that, in so doing, it would deform them and block the development of a European alternative to the Anglo-American model. Thus the boneheads in the Conservative Party who resist every move by Britain towards closer links with Continental Europe are aiding Euro-federalism, while the idealists who long for Britain to become a fully European country are weakening any prospect of Europe following a path of its own.

It is important that Europe should follow such a path. A chorus of earnest transatlantic voices tells us that it is dangerous for Europe and the United States to drift apart and that the trend should be resisted. They are wrong. The present world order, with its single dominant power, is unsustainable. Whatever the ambitions of the Bush administration, the US is ill-fitted – militarily, economically and culturally – for a global imperial role. A new multi-polar world needs a more assertive Europe. Europeans and Americans will both be better off when they accept that the era of US hegemony is over.

To talk of the end of American hegemony in the after-math of the Iraq war may seem paradoxical, but that war demonstrated the limits of American power. The initial military campaign in Iraq was a notable success, but it was conducted as it was because Turkey denied access to the American forces. The Turkish government did this despite huge economic incentives offered by the Americans. It had little choice. The war was so widely and deeply unpopular in Turkey that any other policy posed risks to the regime. There is a conceit in Washington that America can afford to ignore the voice of the street in Muslim countries. Turkey's stance shows that this is a delusion.

The limitations of America's military might are equally clear in the context of post-war Iraq. US policy was based on the conviction that the Iraqi majority wants something like western democracy. Aside from the heavily partisan specula-tion of some Iraqi exiles, there was never much evidence for this belief and events since the war ended have shown it to be baseless. If Iraq's Shia majority wants democracy, it is of an Iranian-style theocratic type, not any western liberal variety. In destroying the Ba'athist state, the Americans not only toppled a brutal tyranny, they also demolished one of the Middle East's most long-standing secular regimes. It seems not to have occurred to them that in these circumstances power would pass to the mullahs. Just as in Europe after the First World War American enthusiasm for self-determination released the evil genie of ethnic nationalism, so today the neo-cons driving US policy in the Middle East are unleashing the suppressed power of radical Islam.

In Iraq the result is to leave the US in a quandary. US forces are not trained to act as an army of occupation. The Pentagon's overriding preoccupation with 'force protection' bars the soldiers from any close contact with the people they claim to have liberated. Against this background, it is not surprising that American forces have resorted to deadly force against peaceful demonstrations. Such incidents are likely to increase as indigenous power structures spring up around the mullahs to deal with the anarchy that has followed the collapse of the Ba'athist regime.

Manifestly, the American military does not possess the skills that are needed in circumstances such as these. Even if it did, it would not have the resources. The Rumsfeld doctrine, supposedly vindicated by the success of the war, demands small, highly mobile forces equipped with the latest technology. This can only mean a reduction in the size of the US army. There will simply not be enough boots on the ground to sustain the messy, colonial-type occupation that will be required.

The attacks of 11 September may have made Americans more ready to tolerate the burdens of war, including a far-reaching curtailment of their liberties. But this does not mean they will accept an unending stream of casualties. Today, as in previous periods, American culture harbours a strong strain of isolationism. Yet a sizeable long-term military presence seems required if the US is to retain control of the country. How else can the emergence of an Iranian-style regime be forestalled and US control of Iraqi oil maintained?

The Bush administration's muddle in Iraq exemplifies a larger incoherence in American thinking. Under the influence of neo-conservative ideologues, the US has embarked on an imperial mission it has neither the means nor the will to sustain. There is nothing new in American imperialism. Despite its anti-colonial self-image, the US has long enjoyed the privileges of empire in Latin America, and it has used its control of transnational institutions such as the IMF to exploit developing countries in classically imperialist fashion.

What is new is the scale of American ambitions. The US is seeking to entrench a uni-polar global regime at a time when its dependency on the rest of the world has never been greater. The theory of American imperial overstretch developed by Yale University's Paul Kennedy in *The Rise and Fall of the Great Powers*, published in 1987, may have been premature, but it was prescient in capturing the mismatch between American imperial ambitions and growing American economic weakness.

The weakness of the dollar shows just how vulnerable the US has become. In part it reflects a belated realization that the claims made for the unique productivity of the American model were largely fraudulent. The scandals revealed at Enron and other American companies were not just examples of corporate excess. They suggest that the extravagant claims that were made for the American model of capitalism in the 1990s may well have relied on cooking the books. If international investors are fleeing the dollar for the euro, one reason is that they suspect that when they bought into American assets in the 1990s, they were robbed.

Besides showing how widely the US economic model is

discredited, the weakness of the dollar is a sign that a multi-polar world is already a reality. Hostility to US Middle Eastern policies may be one reason why the Saudis are diverting some of their resources into Europe. Similarly, resistance to the American-led global monetary regime is clearly a factor in the recent call by the Malaysian prime minister, Mahathir Mohamed, for Malaysia's state oil company to abandon the dollar for the euro. It is worth remembering that Iraq converted its currency reserves from dollars to euros in October 2000. At the time, expert economic opinion was virtually unanimous that this would prove a costly error. In fact, because the euro appreciated hugely, the Iraqi regime made a handsome profit from the exchange. Malaysia may be only the first of a number of countries to follow its example.

The effect of American hubris is to rally resistance to US power, and Europe is pivotal in this global reaction. America may be able to intimidate small states by reminding them of the fate of Yemen, a desperately poor country whose economy was nearly destroyed when the US cut off aid in retaliation for its opposition to the first Gulf war. It cannot bully the EU in quite the same way. Aside from the euro's growing strength, European attitudes on issues of war and peace reflect those of the international community: not the fictitious entity invoked by the US to rubber-stamp its unilateral decisions, but the actual community that forms a majority in every transnational institution.

The US is alone in seeing pre-emptive war as a legitimate instrument of foreign policy. It is not just Europe that finds the peculiar mix of dark Manichaean gloom and wild Pelagian optimism that shapes American policies today alien, repugnant and dangerous. So do Russia, China, India, Japan, much of

Africa and Latin America and the whole of the Islamic world. In speaking up for sober diplomacy against American ranting and bullying, Europe speaks for practically the entire world.

What the world needs is not the healing of Euro-American tensions, as preached by pious Atlanticists, but a European counterweight to American power. The Atlantic Alliance was a by-product of the internecine European conflicts of the twentieth century: two civil wars and an ensuing cold war. Now that those conflicts are past, Europe and America are reverting to what they were in the nineteenth century – civilizations that, despite their common roots, grow in very different directions. Europe and America are divided not only by their diverging economic interests and foreign policies, but also by their values and world-views. I am sure that European perspectives are closer to reality, but no amount of argument will dispel the illusions that animate American foreign policy. Only history can do that.

There are two large obstacles to Europe acting as a brake on US power. The first is Europe itself. Saddled with a currency whose present strength merely compounds its economic problems, deeply divided and yet still wedded to obsolete ideas of top-down harmonization, the EU is as far from being able to act as a coherent and effective force in the world as it has ever been. Internally, it is not exactly a hotbed of progressive forces. In several countries the far right has made a comeback, exploiting the social side-effects of globalization to mount an attack on immigrants and minorities. Militarily, it is still far from developing any operational rapid reaction force, and European governments show little sign of accepting the large increases in defence expenditure that will be necessary if the EU is to have the ability to act independently of the US.

Europe has become the voice of the international community and the euro a viable alternative to the dollar. Yet in terms of projecting its power in the world, the EU is still nowhere near mounting an effective challenge to the US.

The second obstacle is Britain, and more particularly Tony Blair. Here the difficulty is not, as pro-Europeans maintain, the Prime Minister's failure to summon the courage to call a referendum on the euro, and thereby fulfil his ambition of putting Britain at the heart of Europe. The real problem is that if Blair were to take Britain more deeply into Europe, the prospects of the EU developing into a brake on American power, which at present are slight, would be reduced to zero. When he first came to power a number of commentators identified Blair as a European Christian Democrat. If that was ever true, it is no longer. In his view of the world, the Prime Minister is now a fully fledged neo-conservative. He sees American power as the embodiment of progress and views Europe chiefly as an impediment to American policies. If Blair achieves his dream of taking Britain into the heart of Europe the result will be to split the EU irrevocably. On every issue of importance Britain will take the side of the 'new' European countries that are forging bilateral ties with the US. Whenever it can, Britain will thwart the attempts of 'old' Europe to shape the EU into a force distinct from, and capable if necessary of opposing, the US.

So long as it serves a Blairite agenda, Britain's deeper integration into the EU spells the end of any European project worthy of the name. Not only in foreign and defence matters but also in economic and social policy, Britain's goal will be to 'modernize' Europe on an Anglo-American model. Continental Europe will be urged to emulate Britain's public services, a difficult process that might take some time, given that it would mean wrecking the incomparably more user-friendly services they enjoy now. They will be lectured on the virtues of the now largely privatized British pensions, which has left very large numbers facing penury in old age. They will be told to deregulate their communications industries, making it easier for an American view of the world to dominate the media. In short, they will be told to repeat the experience of Britain over the past 20 years, in which it has become a tacky replica of the US.

The much-maligned 'old Europe' will be much better fitted to the emerging multi-polar world than to the backward-looking visions of Atlanticists such as Blair. If Europe has a future, it is as an alternative to the US. If President Chirac really understands this, then – in the spirit of Charles de Gaulle – he will veto Britain's bid for euro membership.

May 19, 2003

22

BLAIR IN RETROSPECT

Tony Blair will never make a mark on history comparable to that left by Margaret Thatcher. Setting out to devise a successor to Thatcherism, he has ended up peddling a pale imitation of it. Thatcher's forced march to modernization has not been followed by a post-Thatcherite project. Instead, aiming to consolidate Thatcher's inheritance, Blair has embarked on a crusade to entrench a revolution that ran out of steam more than a decade ago. His defiant conference speech – 'I can only go one way. I have not got a reverse gear' – may have echoed Margaret Thatcher's 'the lady's not for turning', but there is no parallel between Thatcher's historic impact and Blair's vain aspirations. None the less, just as Thatcher lost power as a result of a revolt in her own party and the public backlash against her hubris, so power is slipping inexorably away from Blair.

It is not that Blair has run out of ideas. He did not need an ideology in order to complete the destruction of the Tories and his lack of one may actually have been an advantage in securing the support of former Conservative voters. Tony Blair is not at risk because Blairism is crumbling away, for no such body of ideas has ever existed. Nor is he vulnerable because he is not trusted, a common disability of politicians, and no great obstacle to success. If Blair fails to make it to the next election, it will be because his judgement has come to be seen as flaky. As the consequences of taking Britain into an unnecessary and unwinnable war become clear, his competence will be increasingly at stake. With a hostile press at his heels, Blair may increasingly appear seriously detached from reality, a perception that proved fatal for Thatcher.

From one angle, Blair's position is stronger than Thatcher's ever was. He has a mountainous majority and the opposition is non-existent. In the 1980s, the split in Labour that issued in the formation of the Social Democratic Party was the single most important factor that ensured Tory hegemony. Even at its worst, however, Labour's condition was not as parlous as the Tories' is today.

The Conservatives were avowedly a party of institutions, but Thatcher's assault on Britain's institutions – the universities, the BBC and the Church of England, as well as the trade unions – alienated them from the Tories and left them open to colonization by Blair. The Tories were the party of the Union, but they have been virtually wiped out in Scotland and Wales, where they survive only by courtesy of an electoral system they derided. The Tories were the party of big business, but the sheer battiness of their campaign against the EU frightened off much of that support, and some of it transferred to Blair. The Tories were the party of the establishment, a position they lost when Thatcher's animus against British institutions became an obsession during her last few years in power. Blair's strategy was to co-opt the institutions and assemble a new establishment, and for a while, it succeeded beyond anyone's hopes.

Stronger than Thatcher in these respects, Blair is strikingly more vulnerable in others. At the time she was toppled, Thatcher was hugely popular in her party, enjoying wide and deep support in the constituencies; even in the cabinet, there were Thatcherite true believers. In contrast, Blair is mistrusted and despised in the constituencies; there is no one in the cabinet on whose support he can count. In his recent attempt at a relaunch he has had to trawl among former cabinet members such as Peter Mandelson, Stephen Byers and Alan Milburn for supporters.

Thatcher did not always have the hard-line free-market convictions with which she came to be identified. Until she became leader of the party, it was hard to distinguish her outlook from that of many other Tory hopefuls of her time; but the world-view she adopted in office chimed with the instincts of much of her party and a pivotal section of the electorate. By contrast, Labour has never warmed to Blair. It tolerated him because it saw him as a winner. Now his increasingly hysterical incantation of the Tina mantra – 'There Is No Alternative' to neo-liberal modernization – is turning off segments of even those parts of the electorate that voted for Thatcher. What is the point of a leader so hopelessly adrift from opinion in his party and the country?

No matter how contrived her media personality may have been, Thatcher embodied the spirit of the age. She understood that the post-war British settlement had broken down irretrievably. True, she was not the first politician to come to that realization. Denis Healey first understood that the Keynesian economic management and corporatist institutions by which Britain had been ruled since the end of the Second World War were no longer viable. But Thatcher was able, where Labour was not, to break with the ruling consensus. The result was a revolutionary shift in British politics. Thatcher's policies had all the blemishes and human costs that go with revolutions, but they represented a genuine break with the past. Who can say the same of Blair's policies?

At a deeper level, Thatcher's vision of Britain was backward-looking. While she boosted an American-style culture of individualism, she harked back to the repressive mores of post-war Britain. Though she rejected the economic settlement that came out of the Second World War, she dreamt of restoring the kind of society that it had produced. But the social conservatism of the 1950s went hand in hand with the post-war economic settlement. The stuffy suburban Arcadia to which Thatcher looked back with such nostalgia was an artefact of Labour government.

The innermost contradiction of Thatcher's project was in its attempt to revolutionize the economy while renewing a society based on the authority of the past. Economic life was to be based on freewheeling choice and the pleasures of unrestrained consumption; family life on duty and stoical restraint. It was an impossible combination, and in the event the conflict proved fatal for Thatcher. Her economic policies accelerated changes in society that left the party she had reshaped in her image redundant. She succeeded in forcing a brutal version of modernization on Britain, but her most lasting legacy may be to have given birth to a country in which her party is irrelevant.

Blair never bewitched his party in the way Thatcher did, and for that reason he has done less damage to it. Unlike the Tories, Labour can renew itself, but only by recognizing that Blair has become a dangerous liability. For all the talk of relaunches and big new ideas, Blair cannot recover his position. The damage has been done, and it is irreversible.

*

Blair himself struck the most fateful blow to his position. When he took Britain to war in Iraq he threw in his lot with George W Bush; but he cannot expect much in the way of gratitude for this gesture. In Washington, he is loathed by the neo-cons for persuading Bush into going the UN route. His constant talk of the need for state-building evokes deep mistrust in American nationalists such as Donald Rumsfeld. There can be no doubt that if Bush's strategists, ruthless pragmatists such as Karl Rove, were to advise him that the war was hurting his presidential chances, he would bring it to an end without hesitation.

As far as Bush is concerned, Iraq is expendable – and so is Tony Blair. The Prime Minister was invaluable to the president in giving the war a veneer of legitimacy. His eloquence in stating the case for war has often been praised, but his lawyerly clarity in fixing on weapons of mass destruction as the chief *casus belli* has only aggravated the administration's difficulties. From being a priceless asset, he is well on the way to becoming an embarrassment.

In Britain, the Hutton inquiry is unlikely to deal the PM a fatal blow, but its cumulative effect can only weaken his position. Its remit may be restricted to examining the circumstances surrounding Dr David Kelly's death, but the inquiry has already shown that, in making the decision to go to war, Blair did not rely on expert judgement about the nature of Saddam Hussein's threat to Britain, if any. He relied instead on his own moral compass. It is this revelation that may ultimately prove most damaging.

Tony Blair's popularity was at its peak when he seemed to be doing little more than intuit the public mood. The chameleon-like skill in being all things to all people that was so useful in opposition also served him well in his first few years in power. During that period, Blair's finely tuned antennae seemed near-faultless. His success during that period may well be related to his not calling on any reserves of personal belief, but simply responding to events.

It is sometimes said that the Prime Minister has no political beliefs, but a better way of describing him is to say that he believes in something other than politics: his own capacity to judge right from wrong. A consummate trimmer in all matters political, Blair is stubborn and reckless on what he takes to be basic issues of morality in international relations. Some may see this as an admirable trait, but it is also a dangerous one when accompanied, as it is in Blair's case, by a simplistic view of the world.

It seems clear that Blair decided early on that he would support US action in Iraq come what may. This decision was justified by geopolitical reasoning – unilateral American action would have dire consequences for the international system, he argued – but it was not long before British support for the Americans acquired the status of an overriding moral imperative for the Prime Minister. Starting as an exercise in realpolitik, his uncompromising support for US policies soon turned into a moral crusade. In effect, Blair staked his political future on the ethical rectitude of Bush's ill-fated adventure in Iraq.

It is here that a genuine parallel can be found with Margaret Thatcher. She, too, identified herself with certain policies, most notably the poll tax, and persuaded herself that only a lack of resolute will stood in the way of their success. Her immovable stance was her undoing, because it created the perception that she had become hubristic and irrational. From that point on, her judgement was no longer trusted. Blair is already in this unhappy position and, as the news from Iraq gets steadily worse, doubts as to his judgement can only grow stronger.

Blair's persona, like Thatcher's, is largely a media construct: from being a fawning Bambi, he has become a weary Caesar – but neither caricature does justice to the complex reality behind the public image. His insistence that he will never deviate from his self-appointed mission to make Labour the vehicle of the orthodoxies of the Thatcher era fails to inspire conviction.

Is it possible that Blair does not understand that history has moved on since Thatcher's time? Or is he laying the ground for his last stand, so that when his message is rejected he can turn his back on his party, a prophet scorned?

At present, Blair resembles John Major more than he does Margaret Thatcher. The recent relaunch is eerily reminiscent of the dog days of the last Major administration, right down to Blair's new campaign (which made the *Sunday Times*'s front page on the eve of the Labour conference) 'to crack down on unnecessary roadworks'.

Major was destroyed by a single decision – to go into the exchange rate mechanism at an unsustainable level. His government went down as one of the worst in British history. So far Blair has not brought his party to such a desperate pass, but it will be downhill all the way for Labour so long as he remains leader.

October 6, 2003

23

LAYING THATCHER'S GHOST

Francis Bacon once remarked that he voted for the right because it makes the best of a bad job. Like many of the painter's observations, it captures a whole way of looking at things, in this case, one that has vanished from politics. The idea that humans are an incorrigibly flawed species is taboo today, but it was the right's key tenet for much of the past 200 years. It was abandoned only in the 1980s, when the Tory party became the vehicle for an anachronistic experiment in reviving nineteenth-century individualism.

The keynote of Margaret Thatcher's outlook was not any insight into human imperfection, but a militant faith in progress. What Britain – and later, as her vision became more hubristic and fantastical, the entire world – needed was a permanent revolution, in which the spirit of capitalism was promoted throughout society. Armed with this bullish philosophy, Thatcher forced a brutal modernization on the country. It was a traumatic process that cost her the leadership and nearly destroyed her party. No Conservative leader after her has been able to slow the party's decline into a rancorous rabble. If John Major was unable to nudge it back into the mainstream, William Hague and Iain Duncan Smith fared no better in their attempts to lead it from the right. With the ties of loyalty severed by a matricidal coup, the party had become ungovernable.

Can Michael Howard succeed where three previous Conservative leaders failed? His emergence as leader has been greeted as a sign that the Tories are regaining their sanity. Howard is a subtle and ruthless politician of vast experience. Unlike his Cambridge contemporary Kenneth Clarke, he shows signs of having reflected on that experience. Assuming that his coronation is unopposed and does not provoke too much anger in the constituencies, he may be able to unify the party and turn it at last into something closer to an effective opposition – but can he take it back to power? His hard-line Thatcherite past may help to endear him to Tory activists, it is often said, but it can hardly enable him to reach out to the floating voters he must attract if he is to lead the party back from the wilderness.

It is sensible to discount the media euphoria surrounding Howard's seemingly effortless rise to power. Recent opinion polls suggest that the Tories face forbidding difficulties, and even now may not have hit the bottom. If Howard fails to deliver the goods in terms of party unity, he will face the wrath of the constituencies, which remain resentful at the way Duncan Smith was removed from power. Even if Howard were to retain the loyalty of his party, it may be at the cost of failing to recoup the voters it lost to new Labour and is now losing to the Liberal Democrats.

It is entirely conceivable that, a couple of years on, the Tories will still be locked in introverted despair, facing a third landslide defeat at the polls.

There is another scenario, however. Howard may turn out

to be the Tory leader who lays Thatcher's ghost. His cast-iron right-wing credentials may enable him to make a decisive break with the party's Thatcherite past, an achievement that has consistently eluded the party's avowed modernizers. If he can do this, he will have a big advantage over Tony Blair's New Labour, which is mired in the defunct orthodoxies of the Thatcher era.

It is commonly thought that the only way the Tories can re-enter the political mainstream is by undergoing a Blair-style transformation. This is a distinctly unpromising strategy for the Tories. It would amount to copying Blair copying Thatcher – hardly a winning gambit at a time when the voters are looking for something very different from the neo-liberal gruel that both parties have served up for the past decade.

Blair's initial success in attracting Tory voters may have come from aping Thatcher, but history has moved on since then. If the imperative for the Tories is to bury their Thatcherite past, re-importing Thatcherism from new Labour is hardly a wise move.

The vision of a 'kinder, gentler' Conservative Party so dear to Tory modernizers is a view of politics from the rear-view mirror. Michael Portillo's fond notion of joining free-market economics with social liberalism may have a certain intellectual charm, but – ironically, given Portillo's past as a man of the hard right – it is a decidedly bien-pensant vision, in which modernization can mean only the continued advance of liberal values. Outside the wine bars and think-tanks of Westminster, this view has little resonance. In contrast, a policy agenda that combines leftish-sounding promises on pensions and university tuition fees with a draconian stance on crime and asylum-seekers could be horribly effective.

If, as seems likely, Howard refines the policies fumblingly initiated under Duncan Smith, he could achieve something that new Labour has signally failed to do, and develop a genuinely post-Thatcherite agenda. Unlike Portillo's rarefied vision, this will not be yet another variation on nineteenth-century individualism. It will be a version of populism embodying a much harsher modernity, in which the power of the state is central.

Many will find this new Tory populism repugnant. Social democrats and Thatcherite true believers alike will be scandalized by this mix of old-left attitudes on public services with social authoritarianism. It is an ugly brew, but anyone who underestimates its potency is making a big mistake. In the chaotic environment produced by accelerating globalization, right-wing populism has every prospect of thriving. Howard's version could enable him to solve the crucial conundrum that has defeated his predecessors: how to attract support among voters at large while retaining that of party loyalists.

Only a few years ago, credulous commentators were talking of a new Gladstonian era of peace and free trade. In a sense, the globalized world that existed before the First World War has returned, but it is far removed from the idealized version propagated by gushing Blairites. Like the late nineteenth century, the early twenty-first century is a time of geopolitical conflict and colonial wars. Control of scarce natural resources is a prime objective of the great powers, and the Great Game is being played again in Central Asia and the Gulf.

In Russia, where the triumph of capitalism was supposed to ensure democracy, a new kind of authoritarianism is emerging. Vladimir Putin's regime is not a lapse into the communist past any more than it is a stop on the way to the glories of western capitalism. It is a new type of government – a hybrid of democracy and tyranny that may well be a model for the twenty-first century.

Advancing globalization is producing a powerful political backlash, not in the confused and ineffectual anti-capitalist movement, but in the mainstream parties. Protectionism is on the rise, notably in the US, where both parties are busy reviving the Yellow Peril. In Europe, immigration has become the central political issue in almost every country, with all parties promising to do anything necessary to stem the flow of asylum-seekers.

Predictably, the political response to the dislocating effects of globalization is a growing demand for strong government. People are turning to the state, not as a guarantor of market choice, but as a buffer against insecurity. Now, as in the past, economic modernization and an activist, often authoritarian, state go together. In the late nineteenth century, it was the Continental European right that first understood this truth. In Britain, more than a hundred years later, it may once again be the right that refashions the modern state. If so, it will not be Gladstone but Bismarck who supplies the model.

New Labour embraced Thatcherite economic policy as a badge of respectability, but it is now a liability. If, as seems certain so long as Blair remains leader, the government clings to the orthodoxies of the 1980s, the political initiative will shift back to the Tories. Like the Thatcherites it has so assiduously copied, new Labour will end as one of history's casualties.

The difficulties facing Howard's leadership are well known. The Conservative Party in the country is old, with an average age in the sixties. Having frightened off donations from big business with its shambolic performance and strident anti-Europeanism, its finances are not in the best shape. With the first-pass-the-post system now tilted heavily against it, it has an electoral mountain to climb if it is to regain power. Contrary to the widely held opinion of liberal commentators, Howard's reputation as an illiberal home secretary may be an asset to him; but it is hard to see how he could go much further in that direction than David Blunkett has gone. Above all, if Howard is crowned the new Tory leader, he must reconcile his party to the need to reach out beyond itself to the centre ground in the country.

This may be a daunting task, but I would not lightly dismiss Howard's chances of pulling it off. It is easy to indulge in wishful thinking about the great British public. True, in some respects, it is notably more tolerant than its leaders. An easy-going attitude to sex is now part of the national character. British culture is lax and hedonistic; it is weaned on debt and soft drugs, and has no memory of Victorian values. But that does not make it liberal. Most voters see no reason why the government should interfere with their pleasures, but they are unforgiving in their attitudes to those they see as law-breakers and outsiders.

Equally, the British public is not now, if it ever was, notably social democratic in its values. It has no time for Thatcherite dogmas on privatization and it resents Blair's Thatcherite policies on higher education, pensions and, perhaps, the NHS. But it is not at all keen on high taxes, and has no fondness for redistribution when it does not benefit the affluent majority. Unlike Thatcher, the public is convinced there is something called society; but by society it means people like itself.

Any party leader seeking to garner the floating vote must be attuned to a mix of attitudes that does not fit easily into existing political categories. It is 'liberal' on sex and drugs, 'reactionary' on immigration and law and order, old Labourish in its view of some public services but grudging in its attitude to the taxes that are needed to pay for them. It may not add up to a pretty picture, but if there is a centre ground in politics, this is it.

The advantage of Howard's populism is that it can appeal to this British majority and at the same time be accepted by the Tory heartlands. It has become fashionable to view Hague with something approaching nostalgia, and certainly by comparison with Duncan Smith he was a leader of genius; but he left the Tories with a deeply damaging form of party democracy. If the procedures he bequeathed for the selection of a party leader succeeded in their immediate goal of denying that prize to Kenneth Clarke, they also enfranchised the most backward-looking section of the party. In so doing, they built into its structure a disabling alienation from the country that Britain has become.

Like his predecessors, Howard must placate the constituencies. His insistence that they be given an opportunity to ratify his emergence as leader shows he understands this fully, but if there is danger for him it is unlikely to come from that quarter. The populist modernization he seems set to impose on his party is very much in tune with the interests and prejudices of its most benighted members. Like most voters, Tory backwoodsmen and women want higher pensions and heavily subsidized university places for their offspring. They will welcome the shift away from Thatcherism that these new policies involve.

The danger to Howard comes more from his parliamentary colleagues, who will find it a wrench to break with the habits of treachery they have formed over many years. The effect of toppling Thatcher was to inject a culture of disloyalty into the Tory party. It is now deeply embedded and may be impossible to uproot.

Still, Howard has a real, perhaps unrepeatable, opportunity to give the Tories another lease of life. His brand of populism seems well suited to a political culture in which success depends on flattering the electorate while mobilizing its baser instincts. Even if, in the end, he fails, he will have made the best of a bad job.

November 10, 2003

24

THE SOCIETY OF THE SPECTACLE REVISITED

Tony Benn and Jeffrey Archer do not have a lot in common. The pious parliamentarian and the flamboyant former Tory party chairman come from very different backgrounds. Their careers are incomparable. Aside from a shared lack of irony, their personalities could hardly be more discrepant. Despite these differences, there is one crucial respect in which they are alike. Each is now marketing his personality and life experience as a media commodity.

Each has published a diary: Archer's covering the first 22 days of his prison sentence, in Belmarsh jail; Benn's the decade from 1991 to 2001. Each has taken to performing a sort of theatrical impersonation of himself: Archer in a play staged not long before he went to prison, in which he appeared as a fictive version of his public persona, itself partly invented, and Benn in a one-man show he is putting on throughout the country, in which he appears with his trademark pipe, mug of tea and inimitably quaint opinions.

Long blurred, the borders between politics and entertainment are now virtually non-existent. It is no longer true, as Enoch Powell claimed, that all political careers end in failure. Rather, failed politicians end up as entertainers. In the current media culture of revelatory diaries and confessional memoirs, kiss-and-tell journalism and voyeuristic television, ex-politicians are no different from anyone else in seeking to turn themselves into marketable commodities. Even more than Tony Benn and Jeffrey Archer, Edwina Currie and Ulrika Jonsson picked up the trappings of celebrity in different worlds; but the fact that one of them was once a politician and the other a television presenter is insignificant in comparison with the use each has made of her past. Each has recycled her life experiences as a commodity and is selling it to a public hungry for the vicarious intimacy that comes from self-exposure in the mass media.

Why the media should have developed in this way is a difficult question, but part of the answer is that the cult of celebrity has become one of the chief drivers of the economy. We are long past the time when the major part of economic activity consisted in the manufacture of industrial commodities. In societies in which affluence can be taken for granted by the majority of people, the core of the economy has come to be entertainment. Cars are still bought as means of transportation and books on the supposition that they may contain useful information, but in each case they are sold on the strength of the new experiences they promise. The chief risk facing such an economy is the mood of boredom that comes with satiety. New experiences become passé even faster than new physical commodities, particularly when, as is commonly the case, there is actually nothing terribly novel about them. Consumer fatigue threatens falling demand; the nemesis of a mode of production that starts to collapse as soon as it can no longer grow.

In an economy driven by the need to manufacture demand,

fame sells everything else. This is most palpably true when anyone can be famous. What is novel about the entertainment economy is that it holds out the prize of fame to everyone. In the past, luxury goods were sold to the masses by linking them with the lifestyles of the famous. Today, it is the belief that anyone can be famous that sustains mass consumption. Celebrity has been made into a sort of People's Lottery, whereby the majority of people are reconciled to the tedium of their daily lives.

The mass media have always had this function. As George Orwell noted, the escapist film extravaganzas created by Hollywood in the Thirties played a significant role in dampening down mass discontent during the Great Depression. Through the spectacle of stardom, Hollywood created a phantasmal parallel world, which compensated for the drab insecurity of everyday life.

The entertainment economy, however, has gone further than Hollywood ever did. It has generated the myth that anyone can be a star. When Andy Warhol remarked that in future everyone would be famous for 15 minutes, he did more than project his own narcissism on to the larger world. He forecast the version of capitalism we have currently reached, in which economic growth is sustained by the popular belief that we can all be winners in the lottery of fame.

It is surprising how few people anticipated the rise of the entertainment economy. Those who did were rarely social theorists or economists, or for that matter academic intellectuals of any variety. Perhaps the most clear-sighted vision of what was to come can be found in the work of J G Ballard, who predicted Ronald Reagan's rise to president in a short story published in 1967, and whose experimental novel *The Atrocity Exhibition* – a visionary anticipation of the role of images of catastrophe and violence in the new media economy – was, astonishingly, first published in 1969. Around the same time, Guy Debord, the most gifted thinker of the group of provocateurs and avant-garde artists who called themselves situationists, developed the theory of the society of the spectacle.

Debord anticipated one of the most curious features of the entertainment economy. Foreseeing a time when roles and identities would be continuously reshuffled in the media, he looked to a future in which the accelerated flow of media imagery would altogether block popular access to the past. In this account, the constant circulation of new fashions does more than sustain demand. It creates a corrupt media surrogate of the 'eternal present' invoked by mystics. In the entertainment economy, the past is systematically erased, while the future is closed off from view. As Debord put it: ' The manufacture of a present where fashion itself, from clothes to music, has come to a halt . . . is achieved by the ceaseless circulation of information, always returning to the same short list of trivialities, passionately proclaimed as major discoveries. Meanwhile, news of what is genuinely important, of what is actually changing, comes rarely, and then in fits and starts.'

As a Marxist, Debord cannot help trying to explain 'the society of the spectacle' in economic terms, but it may well be that the roots of the entertainment economy are cultural. This is George Walden's argument in his translation of Jules Barbey d'Aurevilly's *On Dandyism and George Brummell* (published under the title of *Who's a Dandy?*). In a penetrating analysis of the contemporary scene, Walden argues that the aristocratic cult of dandyism, which the nineteenth-century French writer Jules Barbey examined through the figure of Beau Brummell, has now become a mass movement. As he makes clear in his introductory essay, dandyism is not just a mode of dress. It is an attitude of mind, a philosophy or even a religion, that celebrates impermanence and living for the moment, a wilful detachment from ethical and political concerns, and the cultivated display of a provocative individuality.

In Brummell's time, dandyism was an exclusive cult. The attitudes it expressed were inaccessible to most people. Today, Walden observes, it is the habit of millions. The studied nonchalance of Warhol, the well-rehearsed impassivity of Gilbert and George and the languid stylishness of a pop musician such as Jarvis Cocker are not the privileged affectations of a few media icons. They are the culture of the masses. With the unprecedented increase of leisure and affluence in Britain and other post-industrial societies since the end of the Second World War, the dandyish obsession with clothes and the minutiae of personal appearance has re-emerged. Once confined to a small, self-admiring coterie, it is now one of the dominant trends of the age.

Walden does not attempt a full explanation of this development. As he notes, dandyism is not, as Barbey believed, an unrepeatable feature of aristocratic life in Regency England. It is an attitude to the world that can be found in many times and places. The question is why it has come to be so pervasive today. Walden offers a couple of suggestions. He speculates that the contemporary cult of the dandy may be an attempt to stave off boredom: 'Mass societies,' he writes, 'can be as oppressed by feelings of *taedium vitae* and satiety as aristocracies (more, perhaps, since they are oppressed by their own weight and sameness).' This suggests that the restless quest for novelty in fashion which dandyism expresses may be a reaction against the very condition of security that makes dandyism possible. Walden captures a similar paradox when he identifies Andy Warhol as the prototype of the democratic dandy. Warhol's genius, he writes, 'consisted of glorifying the ordinary, of making celebrities of the people, of dandifying the masses'. Walden concludes: 'Today this means giving mass man what he most needs and desires: an illusion of individuation.' Here Walden follows de Tocqueville in commenting on one of the ironies of modern democracy: when it becomes a mass philosophy, individualism almost inevitably mutates into a new mode of conformism.

The cult of celebrity is a product of the imperatives of the entertainment economy interacting with the values of a democratic society. It is not an aberration, an inexplicable mark of cultural decline that we are at liberty to condemn but have no obligation to understand. Where affluence is the normal condition of the majority of people, continued economic growth depends on manufacturing insatiable needs. This is the mechanism underlying the incessant proliferation of new products, and in itself it is familiar enough; but in the entertainment economy it operates in a new way. Commodities are sold not simply as new products, but as new experiences that will somehow attach themselves uniquely to each consumer. Mass consumption is maintained by breaking up consumers into a multitude of shifting niche markets, each catering to a carefully crafted and continually refined illusion of individuality. This strategy is most highly developed in interactive television programmes such *as Big Brother*, which instil the illusion that

207

celebrity is a universal entitlement that everyone can enjoy if they are lucky enough to be selected by everyone else.

One of the most striking features of the participants in *Big Brother* is their idleness. Aside from relating to one another, they have nothing to do. It is this condition of redundancy, I believe, that is the ultimate source of the culture of celebrity. The trend of the most advanced economies is to render the majority of people superfluous to the production process. That does not mean they are headed for life on the dole. On the contrary, in the economies where this trend is most clearly developed – Britain, for example – something like full employment has been achieved. The distinctive feature of the entertainment economy is not an increase in joblessness, but rather that increasing numbers of people work to keep others, and thereby themselves, amused. The booming markets in every variety of therapy and spirituality, the proliferation of designer drugs and designer religions illustrate the urgency of the impulse to resist the *taedium vitae* of which Walden speaks, and to do so in ways that satisfy the need for an illusion of individuality.

It may well be that the culture of celebrity and the entertainment economy of which it is a part will turn out to be unsustainable. After all, they developed in a period of unparalleled peace and prosperity, when democracy was unchallenged by extremist movements, and continued improvement in the average standard of living could be taken as given. It will not be surprising if they go into retreat when these historically abnormal conditions pass away. Staving off boredom is a pressing need only in rare and privileged times. With war and terrorism, financial collapse and the return of unemployment, more mundane needs come to the fore. Security ceases to be a burden, and the taste for individuality is lost. The chief business of life is subsistence. In such circumstances, the media are likely to revert to supplying simple escapist fantasies, as they did in the Thirties.

For the time being, the economy is geared to the marketing of personal experiences and fantasies. In this carnival of illusions, celebrities are at once alluring ciphers of personal fulfilment and the most fungible of commodities, created and consumed in a mechanical process by the logic of media competition. Inherently transitory, contemporary celebrity consists chiefly in an exchange of privacy for money. It is a harried and servile existence. A life subject to the whims of the media can hardly be described as free. The democratic ethos that is embodied in everyone having the chance of being famous for 15 minutes is a fraud. As Chris Evans is reported to have observed: when you get to the top, you find there is nothing there.

October 28, 2002

INDEX

INDEX